PERFECT PREP

AN INSIDER'S GUIDE TO ACING YOUR COLLEGE INTERVIEW

Ethelyn Geschwind

Perfect Prep
An Insider's Guide to Acing Your College Interview
By Ethelyn Geschwind
Two Twin Press

Published by Two Twin Press, Maplewood, New Jersey
Copyright ©2016 Ethelyn Geschwind
All rights reserved.

Editor: Ben Geschwind

Cover and interior design: Davis Creative, DavisCreative.com

Library of Congress Cataloging-in-Publication Data

Names: Geschwind, Ethelyn.

Title: Perfect prep : an insider's guide to acing your college interview / Ethelyn Geschwind.

Description: Maplewood, New Jersey : Two Twin Press, [2016]

Identifiers: LCCN 2016912790 | ISBN 978-0-9979237-0-4 | ISBN 978-0-9979237-1-1 (Kindle) | ISBN 978-0-9979237-2-8 (ePub)

Subjects: LCSH: Universities and colleges–United States–Admission. | Interviewing–Handbooks, manuals, etc. | College choice–United States.

Classification: LCC LB2351.2 .G47 2016 (print) | LCC LB2351.2 (ebook) | DDC 378.1610973–dc23

To my son, Aytan

May you be perfectly prepared
to ace all your interviews.

Table of Contents

1

Why You Should Read This Book

You're about to walk into your first college interview. This school is your first choice and the pressure is on. "I'll just be myself," you think, "and it will all be fine." You meet the alumna* interviewer and she looks friendly enough. She tells you a little about herself and then asks you a question. You hadn't thought about how to answer that one and now you're stuck. What do you do? What do you say? You start sweating, and it's then that you realize you aren't at all prepared for this interview.

Too often, this is exactly what I have observed as I interviewed more than a hundred students applying to my alma mater, an Ivy League university. It's painfully obvious that they had done nothing to prepare and that almost every question took them by surprise.

During the more than two decades that I've been volunteering for the admissions committee at my alma mater, I have interviewed inner-city high school students and suburban high school students; students from public, private and parochial schools; students who will be the first in their family to attend college; and those who come from a long line of professionals. I've interviewed students from wealthy families and students from poor families; students who are American-born and students born in another country. Describe any high school student, and chances are I've interviewed someone fitting that description.

All these students are just like you. They are excited about going to college and eager to make a good impression. They've put in time and effort to get good grades and worked hard to write strong, convincing essays. What they haven't done is prepare for their interviews.

I find that college applicants are confused about the purpose of an interview and, therefore, how to behave, present themselves and respond to basic, straightforward questions. Despite the dramatic advancement of technology and easier access to information than ever before, I have seen little to no change in students' knowledge and understanding of the interview process.

This book will tell you everything you need to know to ace your college interview. It will tell you how to prepare in advance, research the school, dress appropriately, present yourself well, and what and how to communicate before, during and after an interview—in person, on the phone or via videoconference. It will also guide you in developing a personal statement that will tell the interviewer what makes you unique and special. It will explain what the interviewer is looking for and teach you how to convey, in less than an hour, that you have "it."

This book will show you how to turn good answers into great answers, how to turn good questions into great questions—and how to turn what would have been a "good" interview into a "great" interview. Feel free to share the book with your parents if you want them to offer assistance or help; the Appendix contains some guidance for them, should you want their help.

---

* I use the word "alumni" generically to refer to a group of college graduates, although technically "alumni" refers to a group of male graduates or a group of both male and female graduates, while "alumnae" (pronounced "alumnee") refers to a group of female graduates. When referring to a single graduate I use the word "alum." The correct words to use are "alumnus" for a male graduate and "alumna" for a female graduate. Keep these words in mind when referring to the graduate individually.

2

The interview is alive and well

When I tell people that I help high school seniors ace their college interviews, I often hear, "But colleges don't interview anymore." This is not accurate. While it might be true for large, public universities, the college interview is alive and well and can be an important part of the college admissions process. Here are just a few examples of how colleges approach the admissions interview:

- Virtually every applicant to **Brown** has an alumni interview.
- **MIT** attempts to interview *every* applicant. This school has a robust network of more than 4,500 graduates around the world to meet with applicants in their home area. Applicants who had an interview were ten times more likely to be admitted than those who didn't.
- **Harvard** has more than 15,000 alumni to help recruit students.
- In 2011, **Stanford** went from having no alumni interviews to having all applicants offered an (optional) alumni interview.
- **Muhlenberg College** sends its admissions staff to eighteen major cities across the United States to interview students locally in addition to providing on-campus interviews.
- **Carleton**, **Haverford** and **Wake Forest** are among the many small schools that strongly recommend an interview.
- **Yale** and **Columbia** encourage interviews when available.
- **Johns Hopkins** offers interviews by request.
- **Middlebury College** offers alumni interviews to as many applicants as possible.

As more schools move to test-optional admissions—relying more heavily on transcripts, essays and letters of recommendation—the importance of personal interviews will increase. Don't underestimate the power of the interview.

2

Two Secrets to a Successful Interview

There are two key concepts that are critical to the success of your interview, and yet most people don't know them. They're really quite simple.

The first concept is that the interview is about *you*! Later I'll discuss why you are being interviewed and what the interviewer is looking for, and you'll see that no matter what is going on, the whole process is about *you*. As the interviewer meets with multiple candidates and the admissions committee members consider thousands of applicants, you need to make sure they are clear about what makes you different and what is special about *you*; what differentiates *you* from everyone else and why they should accept *you*.

Now, before you go there, don't even think of suggesting that there is nothing special about you. Every one of us is unique and special and has something wonderful to offer. In Chapter 6—Know Who You Are and What You Want—you will have a chance to define yourself, your interests and your unique character traits. By the end of this book, you will be able to articulate your uniqueness and explain these differentiators to the interviewer.

So, the first big concept for you to keep in mind is *It's about me*. Say it out loud right now: "*IT'S ABOUT ME!*" This phrase will go a long way in helping you stay focused during the interview.

A cautionary statement: While you want to give the interviewer a sense of your accomplishments, you need to be sure not to brag. It's okay to be proud of what you've done, but don't be a show-off.

The second concept is a bit different. It isn't so much to keep you focused as to give you direction. You might think that what I am about to say is obvious, but it isn't. You'd be surprised how many interviewees—whether for college, a job or a professorship—don't follow this one. The direction is: *Answer the question.* Yup, answer the question. When you are asked a specific question, answer it. If the question requires a yes or no answer, then respond with a "yes" or a "no" before elaborating further, if necessary.

Having conducted hundreds of interviews in my career, I continue to be amazed at how many candidates simply don't answer the question. It really isn't that hard. Listen to the question and then ANSWER THE QUESTION. As you put together your complete answer, you can elaborate, expand upon, explain in more detail, or just add to the response, but be sure you answer the question! I can't stress this enough.

When the interviewer asks you to tell him your favorite book, name a book, not an online blog. When he asks you to tell him something about yourself, don't ask, "What do you want to know?" When you are asked to name something you would change about your high school, don't just vent about your high school. Answer the question and say what you would change, and why.

Now let's put the two concepts together. "When I ANSWER THE QUESTION, I need to make sure IT'S ABOUT ME." When you are asked about yourself (and that's typically the point of the interview), talk about yourself. When you are asked about how you would do something, say how *you* would do it. Don't say how "one" might do it or how it "could" be done; say how you, yourself, would do it. When you are asked to describe something *you've* done, describe something you've done, not something someone else has done and not something someone else could do.

CHAPTER SUMMARY

Two Secrets to a Successful Interview
- It's about me!
- Answer the question!

3

Why You Are Being Interviewed

The members of the admissions committee have already received your application. They have seen your grades and read your essays. They have read your teachers' letters of recommendation and have received feedback from your guidance counselor, religious leader and basketball coach.

And yet, they *still* want to meet you. They have asked an alumni volunteer to give up time in their personal life to meet you. They have committees of people in place to coordinate the interviews and to manage the system set up to support the reporting. And, by offering an interview, the admissions committee has given itself yet one more thing to read as part of the admissions process. So why do they do it? What could they possibly hope to learn by meeting you in person? What could they find out about you that all of your written submissions didn't tell them?

What they expect and hope to find is the real you. A college consultant might help you find the right school, decide whom you should ask for a recommendation, suggest how to answer particular application questions and help you write the essay. The fact is that the admissions committee can't really be sure whose words they are reading. They just have to meet you!

They are looking for two simple things: your "presence" and your ability to communicate. Neither of these is truly evident from any paperwork you might have submitted. The interview is their way of finding out what you are like in person and how well you are able to convey your thoughts and ideas.

Presence

What does it mean? It means that you have what it takes to represent yourself and the school well in the world. Presence is about your style, level of confidence and ability to be comfortable with yourself. Good presence tells the interviewer that you can speak for yourself, represent yourself and carry yourself appropriately in a new and public situation.

The Ability to Communicate

What does it mean? It means that you can speak in complete sentences and string sentences together to create paragraphs. It means that you can convey independent thoughts, articulate your ideas, listen to the ideas of others and engage in dialogue, even with people holding differing opinions. Basically, it means that you can have an intelligent conversation.

Can you really learn how to present yourself well and improve your ability to communicate? Some people will tell you, "No way." They'll insist that other than ironing your shirt, you can't really prepare for your college interviews. I disagree.

In helping students prepare for their college interviews, I have proven, time and again, that you can greatly improve your presence and communication skills—and it doesn't take long to get the hang of it. It's simply about body language, focusing on how you speak, looking the interviewer in the eye and being aware of what's going on around you. And it's about taking every opportunity to sell yourself.

Think of a college interview as you would a first date. Think about the things you notice when you are with that other person.

How did he act in public? Did he give thought to what he wore, how he talked to you, or how he described himself? How did he communicate with you? Did you understand each other? Did you make a connection? Did she listen to what you had to say? Did she ask you interesting questions? Did she make you feel that what you were saying was important?

This is what the interviewer will be thinking about when they meet you. You have the opportunity to make a great impression: take advantage of it!

CHAPTER SUMMARY

The Interviewer Wants to See:

- Your presence
- Your ability to communicate

What the Interviewer
Is Looking For

After the interview, the alum submits a written report to the admissions committee that tells them what they observed about you. It might describe the conversation you had, possibly referencing specific things you said—especially those that showed your strengths and your level of interest in the school. Ultimately the interviewer must answer the question, "Do you recommend that this candidate be accepted?" Or, similarly, "Will this student benefit from and contribute to the academic and social experience at this college?"

The detailed write-up is meant to address some basic areas of interest to the admissions committee. The committee members are trying to learn more about your personal traits and characteristics in a way that can't be derived from your application. Some of these characteristics and attributes might have been mentioned by others in your letters of recommendation, but this is another way for the committee to find out what kind of person you are.

Colleges typically look for:

Intellectual Curiosity

Are you an open-minded person? Are you interested in new things, and do you enjoy learning? To what extent are you willing to consider other people's points of view and are you tolerant of others whose points of view might differ from your own? Are you the type of person who will pursue learning and encourage others to do the same? Will you be a positive influence on your classmates—both in and out of the classroom?

Personality

What specific characteristics and qualities do you possess? Are you adaptable, patient, responsible and honest—or are you set in your ways, arrogant, thoughtless and rude? Will you be a positive force on campus or a negative one? How are you likely to treat your professors, roommates and classmates?

Values

What values do you hold dear? Are you a selfless and generous person? Do you put honesty and integrity above all other values? It isn't about being right or wrong but about your personal priorities. The interviewer is looking for actions and examples, whether exhibited or discussed, that reflect those values.

Interests

What do you like to do with your free time? Do you volunteer to help others, or have you focused on being the best at something, such as a sport or other activity? Are you interested in playing video games, connecting with friends through social media, watching movies, camping, writing, etc.? Are you the type of person who typically does things alone or in small groups, or do you prefer being part of a team or a larger group?

Passion

Do you care deeply about something? What makes you come alive? What gets your juices flowing? Do you really want to go to college—and to this college in particular—or are you just going through the motions? Are you enthusiastic about your activities and interests, and do you show excitement when you think about all that college has to offer?

Community Participation

Are you involved in your community, and how might that be displayed or exhibited during your college years? Are you more interested in local issues or global ones? Have you joined a campaign for a social issue? Are you interested in politics? Have you shown an interest in and ability to lead, or are you more comfortable being out of the spotlight and blending in with the crowd?

Maturity

To what extent do you take the initiative? Do you have a sense of social responsibility, and what do you do with your special talents and abilities? How do you respond to your environment and to what's happening around you? Do you think silly pranks are funny, even if they hurt other people? Are you willing to listen to the advice of an elder without arguing or challenging them? Are you responsible; do you hold yourself accountable for your actions, or do you blame others?

You need not worry that the interviewer has unrealistic expectations. They certainly don't expect a teenager to have the maturity of a thirty-year-old, nor do they expect you to have taken the problems of the world on your shoulders. What they do expect is that you have a sense of who you are.

All of this is important as the admissions committee tries to put together a diverse student body. They don't want only class valedictorians, star athletes, leads of school plays or those who volunteer every week in the local food pantry. It's scary to think of a freshman class made up of people with the same characteristics and interests—and that's why the admissions committee works so hard to understand each applicant and his or her unique potential contributions to the new freshman class.

CHAPTER SUMMARY

The Interviewer Is Looking For:

- Intellectual curiosity
- Personality
- Values
- Interests
- Passion
- Community participation
- Maturity

5

Setting Up the Interview

When you apply to college you will be asked to provide an email address and a phone number. You need to use an appropriate email address for this process. If your current one refers to your own sense of self, like stud@hmail.com, or reflects a joke among your friends, like TheBoysClub@hmail.com, it's time to change your address. A simple reference to your name is the most appropriate. You also need to make sure your voicemail is set up and that your outgoing message is clear and friendly. If you've been using a silly or, worse, offensive outgoing message for your friends, change it as soon as you start applying to college.

Some colleges manage the process by sending you the name of the alum assigned to interview you and putting the responsibility on you to contact the person directly. If this is true for a school to which you have applied, be sure to keep your eyes open for the information and contact the person immediately. Make yourself available and keep your schedule flexible. For the other schools, after you've submitted your application you might be contacted to set up an interview. It will likely be an email but might be a phone call.

Email Communications

Remember to check your email on a regular basis, at least daily (and check your junk mail folder as well!). This might sound obvious to some of you, but many high school students don't do this. When you receive an email offering you an interview, make sure to respond, and as quickly as possible.

Contacting a student via email and getting no response is frustrating, and contacting them a second time and not getting a response is even more so. This has happened to me far too many times and is prevalent more and more each year. If and when I did reach the student by phone, the excuses such as "I didn't check my email," "It was in my junk folder" or "I don't have access to that email on my phone" were unacceptable, to say the least.

When you get the email inviting you to have an interview, respond immediately and show a high level of interest and enthusiasm. Make sure you write your response clearly and that you use full sentences and proper punctuation. Don't abbreviate words or use texting shortcuts.

Here's an actual email I received from an applicant:

Hey, this is [NAME] who you just got off the phone with and it would me my pleasure to sit down for an interview with u. I'm very happy that u sent me this e-mail sorry i failed to respond earlier but i honestly feel honored because [SCHOOL] is my number one choice for a College and hope to be accepted....
Please let me know the venue and time of the meeting.

This is a very clear example of what not to do. You might not have caught the typo of "me" instead of "be," but I'm sure you noticed the use of the letter "u" instead of the word "you." Also, the lack of punctuation and capitalization makes it incredibly difficult to read. Again, emails to potential interviewers should not be treated like text messages to friends.

After I followed up to confirm the date, time and location we had agreed to, I received the following email:

This is [NAME] and the location [CAFÉ] is good for me. I'm really looking forward to the interview with u. I just wanna let u know that [SCHOOL] is my first choice college in the list

*of colleges I'm applying and this interview means a lot to me.
Thank you.*

I'm sure you caught the use of the letter "u" again, but did you catch the use of "wanna"? "Wanna" is not a word. After you write an email, go back and read it before you send it. If you don't write well, ask a friend, teacher, sibling or parent to read what you've written before you click send. Everything you do during this process is a reflection of you.

So how do you respond to an email inviting you to interview? An acceptable email response might read as follows:

> *Thank you for contacting me. I am very interested in interviewing and having the opportunity to tell you about myself and to learn more about the school. I am available evenings after 5:00 p.m. and on weekends between 10:00 a.m. and 6:00 p.m. Please let me know what day you have in mind and where you'd like to meet.*

OR

> *Thank you for emailing me about this interview opportunity. I understand that your work schedule limits your availability to certain days and times. I am able to meet next Tuesday at 9:00 p.m. as you offered. Please provide the address of the coffee shop you suggested as well as your mobile number in case I need to reach you before then. Thank you.*

Phone Communications

In a world where phone calls can be ignored, avoided or blocked because the caller is unknown to you, you need to think about answering all calls, even those from unfamiliar numbers. And when you answer the call, be sure to show interest and flexibility. Listen to voicemails as soon as possible and respond as soon as you can.

Try to be accommodating. The interviewer knows that you are in school during the day and likely have after-school and weekend activities or commitments, but keep in mind that he is volunteering his time. If one of your limitations is the availability of a parent or guardian to drive you, be sure to mention that when you are coordinating schedules. It's okay to let the interviewer know that the arrangements and scheduling challenges are out of your control and in no way represent your lack of interest.

Imagine how members of the admissions committee respond when they are told that an applicant didn't reply to emails or voicemail requests to set up an interview. They spent the time to read your application, recommendations and essays—and now you haven't made yourself available for an interview. That's a very clear message to the admissions committee that you wasted their time and aren't interested in attending the school. Don't let this be the reason a school rejects your application.

Scheduling the Appointment

The interviewer will likely suggest some days, times and a place to meet. Even if none of the suggested dates or times works for you, respond immediately. Give alternatives if you can or just let them know you need to see what you can do about securing transportation or rearranging your schedule. The most important thing is to remain flexible.

When you set up an appointment, be clear where you will meet and when. Confirm the time and the address. Exchange cell phone numbers in case you need to contact the interviewer close to the meeting time. He likely has your cell number, so you need to initiate the request for his.

The alum will likely suggest the place to meet. I was surprised to learn that some schools allow, and even recommend, that the interview take place in the alum's home. I don't agree with this recommendation. I suggest that to be safe, you meet in a public place such as a library, coffee shop, café or perhaps the interviewer's place of business.

The location might not be particularly convenient for you, but try to make the suggested location work in order to accommodate the interviewer. I have interviewed as many as ten students in an application cycle, and since I try to conduct the interviews in a short period of time, I might schedule three or four of them back-to-back. If I had to travel around to accommodate all the students, I wouldn't be able to interview nearly as many.

CHAPTER SUMMARY

Keep in Mind When Setting Up the Interview

- Email communications:
  Be responsive and double-check your spelling
- Phone communications:
  Answer the phone; reply immediately; get contact information
- Accommodate the location:
  Be flexible and try to meet the interviewer's needs

FLEXIBILITY IS IMPORTANT!

6

Know Who You Are and What You Want

It's time to create your personal statements. There are some basic categories you can think about to narrow down what's important to you and to explain why this college fits your needs.

Listed below are some major comparisons that could help you articulate what you want and compare it to what the school offers. Review the list and decide which are important to you and which are not. There are no wrong selections to any of the options, so don't be concerned about which you pick. Remember, it's about you and only you!

In a college I want:

- All-male/all-female or co-ed student body
- Small or large class and campus size
- Rural (very remote), suburban (near a city) or urban (in a city) setting
- Specific curriculum requirement or total flexibility of coursework
- Focus on liberal arts, engineering, business, pre-med, fine arts or theater
- Public or private institution
- Optional SAT/ACT test-score reporting
- A stand-alone college (undergraduate only) or one associated with a university (undergraduate and graduate programs)
- On-campus dorms provided

- Off-campus housing available
- A residential campus or mostly commuter campus
- Opportunity to participate in Greek life (fraternities and sororities)
- An historically Black college or one with a high percentage of diverse students
- A particular state or geographic area
- A specific major or academic program not offered by many colleges

As a result of reviewing these categories and considering others, you can formulate your "What I am looking for in a school" statement. It might change over time as you learn more or visit more schools, but you'll need to be able to talk about your preferences during the interview.

Here's what a statement might look like:

I want a relatively small school, located in a major city, offering a strong liberal arts curriculum but tied to a university where taking graduate-level classes is an option. I plan to live on campus and take advantage of campus life. I prefer a school on the East Coast so going home to Virginia is easier, and it also has to offer a degree in zoology.

Or

I want a large, rural school with an engineering program and a strong fraternity network. I want to be able to live off-campus, even in my freshman year, and have total flexibility with the courses I take and the days I attend classes. Having grown up in Virginia, I would like to attend a school in California, or somewhere on the West Coast, to experience a different lifestyle and see what it's like to live elsewhere.

Remember, if you don't yet know what you want, it's okay. And if it changes, that's okay too. But if there is something you really want in a school and the school interviewing you has it, mention to your interviewer that it makes a difference to you. If the school interviewing you doesn't have what you want, you don't have to tell the interviewer.

Now it's your turn:

What I'm looking for in a school is:

_____

_____

_____

_____

_____

Who You Are

Remember how in Chapter 2 we talked about how you have something to offer; how you are unique and any school would be lucky to have you? Now we are going to get into the details.

You might have exceptional test scores and grades, or you might excel at a particular sport or have a special talent for a particular art or activity. But what if you are just "you"? You get good grades, but not the best. You like to play sports but aren't on a team and haven't achieved any exceptional level or accomplishment. You don't play an instrument or sing in the choir. You don't even have a strong interest in a field of study or any idea what you want to do after college.

You are not alone. In fact, you are actually like most of the students applying to college all across America. They know they want to go to college but have no idea what they will study or what they want to be. The thing is, this is what college is all about. Yeah, some students know what they want (or think they do) and jump right into the classes they need for their major. But most are there to be exposed to subjects, thoughts, ideas and people who will help them narrow their search and make their decisions.

So, if you aren't a sports Olympian or a math brainiac, how do you differentiate yourself? How do you help the interviewer understand that you are unique and special; that you have something to offer that no one else can?

Let's look at some basic life-experience categories that might help you begin your self-definition:

- One of many children or an only child
- Oldest, youngest or middle child
- Child of a married or divorced couple
- Child of a single parent
- Child of non-parent guardians
- Have a small or large family
- Have full- and/or half-siblings
- An immigrant or the child of immigrants
- Have lived in many places or just one
- Child of a member of the armed forces / veteran
- Have travelled domestically and/or internationally
- Attend private or parochial (religious) school
- Are religiously observant, very spiritual or an atheist
- Identify with a diverse ethnic group
- Were a Boy Scout or Girl Scout
- Fluent in a foreign language
- Have a disability or special need
- Faced a life challenge
- Have a unique physical ability

Now it's your turn:

The things in my life that make me different are:

_____

_____

_____

_____

_____

What You Like to Do

As you continue with your self-definition, think about how your interests and skills differentiate you from others. Perhaps you're a great writer, have a knack for chemistry or math, are great with animals or children, or have a way of connecting with seniors that no one else seems to have. Perhaps you're good with languages, or at woodworking, coding, knitting or sculpting vegetables. (One young lady I interviewed showed me pictures of flowers that she sculpted from fruits and vegetables, and another gave me a link to a YouTube video of her riding a unicycle.)

Perhaps you love to cook, even if it's just helping your mom or dad around the kitchen. Or you're an awesome bike rider. Or you love nature and like to go camping. Each of us has experiences to share, unique insights and perspectives, and something to offer.

In addition to those listed above, are there other interests you might have? Take a look at the following list and see if you can relate to any of them. Or perhaps you'll think of some of your own. Remember, you don't have to be an expert (most people aren't); you just have to have an interest, a love or a passion for it.

Are you or do you:
- Play a sport
- Play an instrument

- An amateur photographer
- An avid reader
- Play video games
- Skate, ski or snowboard
- Swim, snorkel or scuba dive
- Dance, sing or tell jokes
- A collector—of anything
- Garden or grow flowers
- A movie buff
- Play chess or board games
- A songwriter
- Write/draw comics or graphic novels
- A magician
- Enjoy crossword puzzles, Sudoku puzzles and/or other brain teasers
- Involved in drama productions—on stage or behind the scenes
- Write—prose, poetry, short stories
- Make jewelry for yourself and your friends
- Knit, crochet or do needlepoint
- Listen to music and/or go to concerts
- Ride your bike and perhaps race
- Cook or bake
- Enjoy scrapbooking
- Choreograph dance numbers
- Enjoy model assembly or woodworking
- Paint or sketch
- Other

As you can see, there are many interests a person can have, and you don't have to be the star or expert. You might have checked off one or more than one, while another person has checked off different ones. Are you beginning to understand that you are different and unique? That you have interests and skills that others might not have?

Now it's your turn:

I have an interest in or passion for:

_____

_____

_____

_____

_____

Positive Character Traits

Finally, there are character traits that define a person. Some are positive, some neutral and some downright negative. I've listed some here to help you start thinking about who you are and how you might stand out. In the spirit of being positive, I will focus only on positive character traits.

adaptable	efficient	imaginative	patient
adventurous	empathetic	independent	perceptive
articulate	enthusiastic	innovative	persuasive
aspiring	flexible	insightful	popular
calm	forgiving	intelligent	practical
caring	friendly	intuitive	precise
charismatic	fun-loving	kind	principled
clever	generous	logical	protective
compassionate	gentle	lovable	punctual
conscientious	gracious	mature	rational
considerate	hardworking	methodical	realistic
courageous	helpful	meticulous	reflective
courteous	heroic	modest	relaxed
daring	honest	observant	reliable
decisive	humble	optimistic	resourceful
disciplined	humorous	organized	respectful
dynamic	idealistic	passionate	responsible

romantic	serious	studious	warm
scrupulous	skillful	sympathetic	well-read
selfless	sociable	thorough	well-rounded
self-reliant	sophisticated	tolerant	wise
self-sufficient	spontaneous	trusting	witty
sensitive	steadfast	understanding	
sentimental	strong	vivacious	

Think about which of these adjectives describe you and think of ways you exhibit these traits. For example:

- I am **reliable**. Whenever my next-door neighbors go on vacation they ask me to feed their turtle.

- I am **self-sufficient**. Since my parents work in the evenings, I have to prepare dinner for my younger siblings and myself.

- I am **imaginative**. I have come up with songs and stories to tell my younger sister when I put her to bed.

- I am **organized** and **resourceful**. With the assistance of a family friend I developed a detailed sales strategy and sold more Girl Scout cookies than anyone else in my troop.

- I am **responsible**. As the child of immigrants who do not speak English, I coordinate parent/teacher meetings for my parents and make sure permission slips are signed for my younger brother and sister.

Now it's your turn:

Pick a few adjectives and give examples of how you exhibit that trait or characteristic.

I am _____ .

_____

_____

_____

_____ .

I am _____ .

_____

_____

_____

_____ .

I am _____ .

_____

_____

_____

_____ .

Take the time to go through the list and give examples of as many as you can. You can then use this list to draw on for answers to the interviewer's questions.

There is so much you can tell about yourself by simply telling stories that include your life and family situation, your interests and experiences, and the special things you do or say. This is not the time to be modest; look at yourself and celebrate who you are.

CHAPTER SUMMARY

Create Your Personal Statements
- What you want
- Who you are
- What you like to do
- Your positive character traits

7

Preparing for the Interview

What happens if you are going for a college interview but, in reality, have no idea if you even want to go to that school? Have no idea what you are looking for in a college or what you want to major in? You checked some boxes on the application because you had to, but you really don't have a clue. Sound familiar? You are not alone and need not worry; you can still ace the interview.

The most important thing to do to prepare for your interview is to learn everything you can about the school. Be familiar with the school's history and traditions as well as the "culture" of the school. Use the school's website and any other resources available. Speak to any alumni you might know or students currently attending the school. If at all possible, visit the school and get a tour. For colleges that are close to home, a campus tour is a must. If you live within two hours of a school and don't visit the school, the admissions committee can only assume you don't really want to attend. When you visit the school, meet the students, check out the surrounding area and see what the academic buildings, classrooms, dormitories and other facilities are like.

Do Your Research

In doing your college research, study the school's website and browse through the coursework, especially any generally required classes or ones in your specific area of interest. Know the school statistics and how the school compares with others that are similar in terms of academic reputation, size, location, etc.

You want to be sure that when you walk into the interview, you know as much about the school as possible and what opportunities you would want to take advantage of there. Too often I interviewed students who knew very little about the school. They clearly did no research, which indicates a lack of interest. One student I interviewed spent more of his time researching me than he did researching the school. He knew about me from his Google search but knew very little about what the school had to offer. Spend your time learning about the school, not about the interviewer. Come prepared. Know the school.

Find out the major facts, figures and differentiators of the school. For example, you should know:

- What the school is known for (is it a liberal arts school, or does it focus more on science and engineering?)
- What curriculum is offered (and what is not offered)
- Where the school is located
- The size, diversity and gender make-up of the recent freshman class and of the total college
- The academic degrees that the school offers

Think about all the questions you have and the things you want to know, and look for the answers on the school's website. If you've done the proper research, you'll be able to impress the interviewer with how much you know, which demonstrates your interest in the school.

In addition to all the research you do, find out about any particular programs offered that help with the school's comparative ranking. Know what stands out about the school and what makes it different. You'll want to bring this up during the interview, assuming the program or activity interests you. If the school offers or represents something that is important to you, you'll want to be able to talk about it. For example:

- Goucher College students must complete at least one study-abroad experience and/or an off-campus internship.
- Grinnell College students must follow the motto "service before self." The school has the highest rate of Peace Corps volunteers of any college in the nation. It also has a ten-to-one faculty ratio.
- Cornell College, in Iowa, divides the academic year into eight terms, each three-and-a-half-weeks long. Students take only one course at a time.
- The University of San Diego is a smoke- and tobacco-free campus.
- Rice University has a puppy room dedicated to pet therapy for students during finals.
- Oberlin College's art museum rents out original paintings from the greats, such as Renoir, Picasso and Pollock, to its students for $5 a semester.
- St. Olaf College requires students to complete nearly twenty different courses. It also sends more students abroad than nearly any other school in the United States.
- Rhodes College boasts small classes and emphasizes writing and research. Students are encouraged to participate in service activities and off-campus research.

Take Your Kit

Now that the interview is approaching, it's time to put together your interview "kit." Your kit will have a notebook / pad of paper, a pen and any other personal information you care to share, such as your résumé, along with a list of questions you plan to ask your interviewer. More about that later.

If you are planning to bring along things for your interviewer to see, such as your résumé or your grades or a list of awards, don't be surprised if she puts these things aside. The interviewer is there to talk to you, not to look at test scores, a write-up of your research project or anything else for that matter. Feel free to bring these things with you and leave them behind, but don't get offended if the interviewer doesn't ask you about them.

As you put your kit together, make sure all your written material is perfect. This includes paying attention to typos, grammar, sentence structure—everything. These documents are as much a part of your presence as the clothes you wear (more on that later). Don't hesitate to ask other people for help and to read whatever you have written. Absolutely do not rely on spell check. On one résumé I received from an executive recruiter, the candidate had written that she had helped a company "process there payments" more quickly and efficiently. Obviously, spell check didn't stop her from using "there" instead of "their."

Prepare for the Questions

Part of your preparation will be to develop answers to questions you might be asked during the interview. Lucky for you, in Chapter 11 I've listed the most common questions, with examples of bad answers, good answers and great answers for each. You will prepare for your interview by deciding how you should answer each of these questions, in case they are asked.

You will collect your thoughts around the answers to each question and prepare your oral response. That means you will not only *think* about what you will say, you will practice saying it *out loud,* to another person—a friend, a parent, another relative. There is a big difference between what you say to yourself in your head and what you say to someone else out loud.

During your interview, you will need to focus on the speed of your speech. Many people tend to speak quickly and, depending upon who is listening, might not be easily understood. Part of the practicing you will do is speaking slowly and clearly. As slowly as you think you're talking, talk more slowly. I have interviewed students who not only spoke quickly but also went off on tangents, making it nearly impossible for me to keep track of what they were saying.

CHAPTER SUMMARY

Be Prepared for the Interview

- Do your research
- Assemble your interview kit
- Think about the answers to the questions
- Practice answering the questions out loud

Dress for Success

Over the years, I've had students come to their interviews wearing anything from a suit and tie to a tee shirt and jeans—or worse, leggings, gym clothes or other inappropriate attire. I'm sure you can guess which ones I thought actually cared about making a good impression. I have so often wanted to ask the poorly dressed applicants, "Couldn't you put on a nice pair of pants and a nice shirt?" But I didn't. Instead, I made a note to myself that these applicants were not serious about their application and didn't give this interview much thought.

For the record, the students who dressed poorly were the same ones who were unprepared and tried to fake their way through the interview. The students who came well-dressed were the ones who had prepared and were clearly trying to impress me; those are the students I remember best.

The bottom line is that wherever you are meeting for the interview, you should be dressed for success. Just as you have shown respect to the interviewer in the way you responded to their note, accommodated their schedule, and prepared your questions and answers, you need to show the same respect and prepare what you wear. You need to dress like you gave it some thought and not like you just ran out of the house.

I have been told that nowadays it's okay for a student to wear jeans on an interview; that dressing up makes the student look like they are trying too hard. My response is that you can't try too hard to make a good impression. You'd better hope you don't get someone like me, who expects you to be putting your best foot forward. It's so easy to put on a pair of khakis or slacks instead of a pair of jeans, so why not do it? A young woman can just as easily put on a pair of pants instead of leggings or sweat pants. Take the time to consider how you dress and how you look. When I interview students, I think about how I'm presenting myself, as I represent the school. I would like to see these prospective college students present themselves similarly, as a representation of the best they can be.

In general, you want to wear a nice, comfortable outfit. Think about the entire outfit and care for each part of your appearance, from head to toe. The idea is not to be dressed "perfectly," but to present yourself as someone who wants to make a good impression. This means caring not only for what you wear but also your hair, your nails and your jewelry. So, let's start at the top and work our way down.

Hair

For both men and women, your hair should be clean (oh, the stories I could tell), combed/brushed and neat. That means it isn't in your eyes and you aren't constantly throwing it over your shoulders. Men, if your hair is long, tie it up and get it out of the way. Either be clean-shaven or make sure you have trimmed your facial hair and it looks neat.

Shirt/Top

Men should wear shirts that are clean, neat, collared—preferably button-down—and ironed. You don't need to wear a tie or a jacket, but you can consider wearing them depending on where the interview is taking place. Women can simply wear a dress, but if you wear a top it needs to be clean and neat. This can be a blouse, sweater or shirt but nothing too flashy, shiny or distracting. Don't wear anything too low-cut or tight, and don't wear a tank top or spaghetti straps. These will just be a potential distraction to the interviewer, whether male or female.

Pants/Skirt/Dress

Men can wear casual and comfortable pants. Khakis are fine, as are corduroys and wool pants. Again, I don't suggest jeans, but if you must wear them, be sure they are clean, not ripped and not overly worn.

For women, as with men, I don't suggest jeans, but if you must wear them, follow the same guidelines. If you wear a dress or a skirt, make sure it isn't too short; modesty is encouraged in this situation.

Some guidance counselors tell the students to dress in a manner that is appropriate for the meeting place. If you are meeting at a coffee shop, one might think that jeans are fine. The same is true for the library or the diner. That might be appropriate dress for these locations, but it doesn't mean it's appropriate for the meeting that will be part of the determination as to whether you'll be going to the college of your choice.

Accessories

Take the same care with your accessories as you do with your clothes. Men, wear a belt; make sure that it isn't worn or frayed and that the buckle covers the button or snap on your pants. Women, wear a belt as appropriate for the outfit.

For women (and men) who wear nail polish and jewelry, don't put on anything flashy that will be distracting to the interviewer. While you might like the black nail polish or think that the bright red looks great on you, you don't want the interviewer watching your hands instead of listening to you. Your best option is to go neutral on color. Jewelry should also be neutral, with no big earrings and no bangle bracelets banging on the table.

Body Art

Tattoos are an expression of yourself and can be beautiful. But while tattoos can be large and colorful, or small and subtle, they can also be distracting to an interviewer. If you think your tattoo(s) will give the wrong impression or be too distracting, cover them up using a collared and long-sleeved shirt. The same is true for body piercings. Tone it down, if you can. I am not suggesting you change who you are, your beliefs or how you see your body. What I am suggesting is that you present yourself in the best light possible, keeping in mind that not everyone is interested in tattoos and piercings. The best approach is to be neutral.

However, if who you are is defined by your tattoos and/or piercings, by all means don't hide them; show them off proudly and talk about them. But if they aren't what defines you, or you don't want them to be, cover up or remove whatever you can before the interview.

Shoes

The one thing people most often forget to care for when preparing themselves for an interview is their shoes. They should be clean and polished and preferably without holes. For men I suggest dress or semi-dress shoes, appropriate with your outfit, but no sneakers, if possible. And for women I suggest comfortable shoes with no or low heals and no sneakers, if possible.

Keep in mind that what you wear to the interview is a reflection of who you are and how serious you are about attending this school. Take the time to dress appropriately and show the interviewer that you have respect for them and the time they are giving you.

CHAPTER SUMMARY

Dress for Success

Pay attention to your:
- Hair
- Shirt/top
- Pants/skirt/dress
- Accessories
- Body art
- Shoes

9

Interview DOs

Now that you've done your preparation and are ready to go, let's cover the basic must-dos of an interview.

Arrive on Time

The interviewer should not have to wait for you. When I sit and wait for a student who arrives late without having called me, I categorize him as irresponsible and rude. Once I had been waiting for a student for ten minutes and, concerned that something might have happened or that he was lost, I called his cell phone. He told me that he and his mom got a late start and he would be arriving within a few minutes. His mom was driving, which meant he could have easily called or texted me at the beginning of or during the trip to let me know he'd be arriving late. By the time I called him, no matter what reason or excuse he might have given me, there was nothing he could say that would justify his disrespect for my time.

I typically schedule multiple interviews on a given day, one hour apart. Since interviews usually last between thirty and forty-five minutes, this schedule enables me to speak to the candidate a bit longer if I need to and provides a slight break between meeting candidates, giving me time to add to my notes, if necessary. So, having a candidate arrive late and disrupt my pattern and flow will interfere with my ability to give that student a fair and comfortable interview and possibly take time away from another candidate. Finally, there is the concern that a late-arriving student runs into the next candidate at the door.

When coordinating your trip to the interview location, consider a plan to arrive early. This is most important for people who tend to arrive late to everything. If it typically takes you longer to get somewhere than you think it should, be sure to leave plenty of time to travel.

To the extent possible, try to be acquainted with the town, location, building and floor where your interview will take place. If you aren't, be sure to leave plenty of time to get there and find the location. If you are going to an office building, you might need to park in a designated area and sign in after showing ID. If so, be sure to leave plenty of time to do all of that and not be rushed. If you're going to a library or coffee shop, it might take some time to find each other or to find an appropriate quiet corner for your meeting.

You might also consider confirming your appointment the day before, which shows responsibility and consideration. A candidate who sent an email to confirm that we were meeting the next day at a particular time got my confirming reply and my appreciation. I knew even before our meeting that he was responsible and understood the importance of a commitment, and I was assured that he would show up.

When you have your interview, your parent or guardian need not—in fact should not—be seen or heard, even if they have driven you to the interview. This interview is not about them. For a campus interview, the parents can be around but won't be in the interview. And so, more than ever, understand the importance of "It's about me." Your parents won't be there to talk about you; you'll need to do that yourself.

Relax

You are likely to be nervous when you head into your interview. I've had students who could barely speak because they were so nervous. I've seen applicants sweat and I've seen them get flustered. Don't worry if any of this happens; the interviewer fully expects you to be nervous.

I advise students that before they step into their interview, they should take two really deep breaths. This is sometimes enough to calm their nerves. If this approach doesn't work for you and you think that your anxiety level will get in the way of your ability to do your very best on the interview, you might consider some different relaxation techniques. Simple things you can do right before your interview are:

- **Be here now** – focus on your body and your senses and only on what is going on at that specific time. Enjoy and appreciate the comfortable car ride to the interview, take pride in your self-assured walk to the location, and experience your pride when you confidently shake the interviewer's hand.

- **Laugh out loud** – a good, hearty belly laugh can lower your stress level and improve your mood. Tell funny stories on the way to the interview or just remind yourself of something amusing as you approach the location.

- **Smile** – yes, just smiling can reduce your stress level. Think about how well you've prepared for this interview and smile as you appreciate all the work you've done.

- **Listen to music** – music that calms you and allows you to enjoy and appreciate the voices, the instruments and the melody. Crank it up in the car or put on your headphones and listen to a song.

- **Sing out loud** – yet another thing that will improve your mood. Belt it out in the car when you listen to that music. Sing out loud as you walk to the interview. And don't worry about what other people think; you'll probably get them to smile and improve their mood as well.

47

Whatever approach you take to relieve stress, don't forget to remind yourself that you have done everything possible to prepare for this interview and are ready for anything the interviewer throws your way.

Greet the Interviewer

Now it's time to meet your interviewer. If they enter the library/café/diner after you have arrived and you are already seated, stand up. This applies regardless of their gender or yours; it is simply a sign of respect. Stand with a straight back and your head up high showing a sense of pride, maturity and confidence and extend your hand to shake. Warning: Don't even think of giving a soft, wimpy handshake to a woman. It's truly offensive to treat a woman as if she can't handle a firm grip; it doesn't speak well for your opinion of her. By the way, women, get rid of your soft, limp handshake if you have one.

While you are shaking the interviewer's hand, introduce yourself, stating your full name. If your name is unique or difficult to pronounce, this is the time to let the interviewer know how to pronounce it properly. From the moment you meet the person, make eye contact. I'm not suggesting you engage in a staring contest, but make sure you look at the person when you are talking to them. Don't look down or over their shoulder and don't talk to the table or your hands. Look at them directly. You can practice this with your friends and family.

Speak Slowly and Clearly

Throughout the interview, speak slowly and clearly, enunciate your words and be careful not to mumble. Speaking slowly has several benefits. First, it allows the interviewer to understand what you are saying. Second, it gives you a chance to pause as you speak and get your thoughts together. This will help you avoid saying "like," "um" and "I mean." When you practice answering questions, out loud, you need to practice speaking slowly. If you typically speak quickly, practice slowing down. And if you think you've slowed down enough, slow down some more. If you speak very quickly or mumble your words, it's likely the interviewer will lose patience and you'll lose their attention. No one wants to have to work hard just to listen. When I interview fast talkers, I leave the interview exhausted.

Be Confident

During the interview, you need to engage the interviewer in conversation. Speak with a loud, clear voice; now is not the time to whisper. If the meeting place has a lot of background noise, make sure to compensate for this by speaking more loudly and clearly. If you are shy, you need to do your best to get over it and be more "forceful" than you are normally comfortable being.

Answer the Question!

Remember in Chapter 2 we talked about the two big secrets— "It's about me" and "Answer the question"? During your interview, remember to listen to the question and answer it. I have conducted so many interviews—for admission to college, for a job and even for PhD candidates who will be future professors—and in each one of these situations, I have had candidates simply ignore the question. In my experience, it was nervousness and a lack of preparation that led to this response. The applicant didn't really listen to the question, and so they answered what they thought was being asked.

When you are being asked the questions, be sure to listen carefully; there is no need to say anything while the question is being asked. You don't need to say "okay." You don't need to nod or show agreement. You don't need to compliment the interviewer on a good, or great, question. You only need to listen; it's that simple.

Talk About Yourself – "It's About Me"

When you are asked about your school, talk about your school. And when you are asked about yourself, talk about yourself. Remember, "It's about me." During the interview, while you can refer to the class, or the team, don't forget to talk about yourself and your role in the success of that class or team. What you are all about, including your strengths and accomplishments, is what the interviewer came to hear. They want to know what you think and why. They want to know how you see yourself and your place in the community and the world.

During the interview remember to stay focused on what makes you different from anyone else they might interview. Remember, "It's about me." What is it about you that you want the interviewer to know? Since this is a supplement to your application and essay, think about something you might not have already mentioned to the school. It might be something you find beautiful, something you can do that has to be seen in person, or some special skill you have.

To be able to determine how you'll fit in, the admissions committee needs to know what you will bring with you to college, other than your charming wit and endearing personality. What will you, as a person, contribute to the school? Whatever it is, you need to stress how it complements or adds to what the school already has or fills a gap or contributes to something that is lacking.

Answer open-ended questions (and most of the questions are open-ended) with information that focuses on you because, "It's about me." You want to be sure that every answer you give focuses on you and what makes you different.

Be Positive

When you answer questions, and even when you ask questions, be positive. Don't trash or speak poorly of other colleges or of your high school. Focus on the good, not the bad. You want to reflect a positive attitude to the interviewer and not be seen as a complainer. If you do think negatively about something and want to address it, you can begin by saying, for example, "An improvement to my high school's course offerings would be the addition of an AP calculus class." This is preferable to saying, "My high school is terrible because it doesn't offer AP calculus."

During your time with the interviewer, stress your strengths and skills and highlight those that make you unique. Using action verbs, such as "lead" and "manage," demonstrates confidence and maturity. Using words such as "empower" or "teamwork" can convey how you help others and meld with a group. Using words such as "accomplish" or "appreciate" shows your positive attitude and can-do approach to things.

Some interviewers want to see how you handle certain situations. They might disagree with something you've said, just to see how you respond or they might actually disagree with something you said. No matter what the conversation, always be polite and respectful. You can think anything you want about the interviewer, but your words and deeds must always be respectful.

CHAPTER SUMMARY

Interview DOs

- Relax
- Greet the interviewer
- Speak slowly and clearly
- Be confident
- Answer the question
- Talk about yourself
- Be positive

10

Interview DON'Ts

Alumni interviewers agree that there are some things you should never do during your interview. Here are some of the major ones.

Don't Say That Another School Is Your First Choice

One measure of college admissions performance is the "yield rate," i.e., the percentage of students who actually enroll in a college after being accepted. A high yield rate means that the college did well in its selection and admitted the best candidates who actually want to attend the school. The higher the yield rate, the more students will want to go there in the future. Some college-rating services use the yield rate as a measure of selectivity. Therefore, expressing a high level of interest is very important to the admissions committee; they certainly won't be inclined to accept someone they know will likely turn down their offer. If they accept you and you decline the offer, the committee must return to the waiting list for another candidate.

When the interviewer asks you where you really want to go to college, don't tell them your first choice is another school. This might seem pretty obvious to some of you, but you'd be surprised how many students didn't answer my question with the name of my alma mater.

If the school you're interviewing for is your first choice, by all means say so. If there is another school that you are favoring, you need not tell the interviewer that you really want to go somewhere else. You can tell the interviewer that you are still seriously considering two (or three) schools and that this one is on that list. If finances play a role in your decision, you can certainly point out that while the school is a preferred one on your list, scholarships and financial aid will play a part in your decision. But don't tell them you absolutely, positively want to go somewhere else.

Don't Tell the Interviewer That the School Is Your "Safety"

If you tell the interviewer that this is the school that you think will absolutely accept you, you are pretty much saying that if any other school accepts you, you will attend that other school. Think about it; why would the interviewer recommend you for admission? If the school is low on your preferred list and you don't want to say otherwise, you can say that you are still in decision mode, are evaluating the different factors, and that this school certainly has what you are looking for in a college.

Don't Lie

Don't, under any circumstances, make anything up. If you don't know something, it's okay to say "I don't know." If the interviewer asks you something specific about the school, something she expects you to know but you don't, don't lie. Rather than say, "I don't know," you can say, "I remember seeing that information on the website but can't recall it offhand." Or, "I didn't do my research on that topic but I would like to hear your perspective and input." Remember, keep everything positive.

A young lady I interviewed told me she wanted to be a pharmacist. When I asked about the required schooling for this profession, she told me it was only a bachelor's degree. Now, even I know that isn't correct. When I asked if the school (my alma mater) offered an undergraduate degree in pharmacy, she told me it did. She was wrong. Busted. I did not recommend this student for admission.

Don't Ramble or Babble

Don't speak in stream-of-consciousness mode with tangential, unrelated information. The interviewer does not want to hear about your sick grandfather's nursing aide who has been taking care of him for years. I know I didn't when the applicant told me all about her.

Don't use words or phrases such as "like," "I mean," "um," "I don't know" or "I guess." Not saying the first three will take practice, as you probably say them all the time. Don't start a sentence with, "To be honest." It begs the question, "Have you been dishonest until now?"

Practice improving your speech by speaking to your family and friends more slowly and asking them to look out for those words. If you become aware of these habits, you'll be able to stop them. Instead of "I don't know," perhaps you can point out that you haven't yet had the experience or the opportunity to know whatever it is they are asking about.

Don't Make Up Questions

Don't make up pointless questions or ask questions about something you could have looked up on the school website. Here are examples of actual questions I've been asked:

- What is the size of the student body?
- Where is the school located and does it have satellite campuses?
- What classes are offered in my major?
- Will I have a roommate when I'm assigned to a dorm?
- What electives can I take?
- Is there diversity among the students?
- Is there a study-abroad program?

All of these questions could have been answered by looking at the school website.

CHAPTER SUMMARY

Interview DON'Ts

- Don't say you'd rather go to another school
- Don't say the school is your safety
- Don't lie
- Don't ramble or babble
- Don't make up pointless questions or ones to which the answers are readily available

11

The Interview

The alum interviewing you will know very little about you. While the amount of information given to interviewers varies by school, they will likely only know the name of your high school, the town in which you live, your areas of interest (extra-curricular activities) and information about your selected major or concentration. They won't have seen your grades, your application, your essay or anything else you might have submitted as part of your application.

Expect the interview to last about thirty to forty-five minutes, although it could last longer. I have heard of interviews lasting two hours, but that is the rare exception.

Don't be surprised if the interviewer takes notes. Because most interviewers accept multiple assignments per admission cycle, they might need to take notes to help themselves remember you. By differentiating yourself, you'll give them something amazing to write down.

Remember your focus, "It's about me." Always keep in mind that you are the only person there to talk about and represent you. Your speech should reflect the pride and confidence you have in yourself. Show a high level of quality in all that you do, including speaking.

The Questions

Each interviewer has his or her own style, of course, but there are some questions that are relatively standard for the college interview. Many of the questions will likely be open-ended and allow for a broad range of responses; these are not simple "yes" or "no" questions. While I'm sure you'll be able to come up with a good answer for each one, I'm going to show you how to turn it into a great answer; how to tell a story filled with all the things you want the interviewer to know and that will hold their attention because the story is interesting and flows well.

Here's an example. I coached a student who was into robotics, and we were working on an answer to a simple open-ended question, "Tell me about your favorite robotics project." It could have been asked as, "Tell me about the robotics project of which you are most proud."

Let's start with two bad answers:

1. I really don't have any favorites; they are all great.

2. The club has built some great robots over the years and I'm proud of all of them.

Next, two good answers:

1. There are a few robots that I have built with my club that were very successful and very complex. My favorite one is the one we called Alice, because she could move around and pick up all the blocks.

2. While it's hard to pick a favorite, the one I made for a boy in a wheelchair is the one of which I am proudest, so I'd have to say it was my favorite.

Now an example of a great answer:

The robotics project of which I'm proudest is one in which I helped build a robot for a child with cerebral palsy, which enabled him to play video games with his brothers. I've been volunteering at the cerebral palsy center of Massachusetts, and over the years I befriended a young man, Joey, who is confined to a wheelchair. I noticed that when his brothers played video games he felt left out. I worked with the other members of my robotics club, of which I am founder and president, and we challenged each other to find a way for Joey to play with his brothers. We came up with a switch that enables Joey to turn the television on and off despite his handicap. The look of happiness and joy on Joey's face when we installed the unit told me that we had done something very special. That robotics project, while small and not overly complex, is my favorite project and the one of which I'm proudest.

See what we did here? We turned a simple answer into a story full of great information about you. We brought together a volunteer activity with teamwork and leadership and compassion. And all we did was tell a story. Good to great.

10 Commonly Asked Questions—and Answers

Here are the most common, typical college interview questions with examples of bad answers (most are actual answers I received during interviews), good answers and great answers. You can find more questions and answers in the Appendix.

#1 Tell me about yourself.

This question is a gift because you don't get more open-ended than this!

Bad Answer: What do you want to know?

If there were something specific the interviewer wanted to know, he would have asked you. Instead, he is giving you the opportunity to tell him whatever you want.

Bad Answer: That's a really big question.

Bad Answer: I like math and science and robotics.

Good Answer: I like history and do very well in my language arts and social studies classes. I have two brothers who are both older than me; they are both away at college. I like to play sports, especially basketball, and I play the piano.

Great Answer: I grew up in the inner city and was home-schooled starting in sixth grade. My five older brothers and sisters were also home schooled. Being part of such a large family has had its advantages and disadvantages. I know how to cook and clean and take care of myself. I also know how to get along with others and take responsibility because in my house we all have to chip in and help. I love to read and take walks, probably because these activities gave me private time when I was growing up. I especially like reading historical fiction focused on foreign countries and cultures. It's this upbringing that has led me to want a large school in a rural area. I am looking forward to meeting students from around the country and around the world, but I plan to request a single when I'm selecting a dorm room. It will be the first time in my life that I have my own room.

In this answer you talk about how your upbringing had an impact on who you are and how it has led to your interests and what you are looking for in a school.

#2 What will you miss most when you go off to college?

Bad Answer: My sister.

Bad Answer: My friends.

Bad Answer: My dog.

These answers are "bad" not only because they are very brief but because they do nothing to show who you are, what you value or how you see yourself in the world.

Good Answer: I will miss being able to go to church with my family each Sunday. We've been going together weekly since I was born, and it has taught me the importance of community and strengthened my commitment to my religion.

Great Answer: I have a strong commitment to my religion, and every Sunday my family and I go to church together. As a result, I have strong ties to the community. I plan to take a religion class in order to learn about other religions, and I'm looking forward to learning about the other students' traditions and practices. The biggest change for me when I go to college will be going to a different church than I've attended my whole life. But I expect this to also be a learning experience. So, the thing I will miss most when I go off to college is going to church with my family each week, but I plan to replace that tradition with a new one of my own making.

In this answer you talk about your commitment to community, your curiosity and your interests. You describe what you would miss, but you also show maturity in how you would manage the change you foresee.

#3 What makes you anxious about going to college?

Bad Answer: Leaving home for the first time.

Bad Answer: Being away from my friends.

Bad Answer: The workload.

Bad Answer: Having to manage my time.

These "bad" answers focus on the negative you see in the situation, rather than taking the opportunity to show the positive and how you plan to deal with the anxiety.

Good Answer: I'm nervous because I will have to manage the workload and because I will be trying to make new friends. In high school I balanced my classes and homework, but I was able to rely on my friends for help and support. In the beginning I'll need to be more focused on balancing academics and my social life, but in time I know I'll be okay.

Great Answer: One of the reasons I'm a bit anxious about going to college is that it will be the first time in my life that I will be away from my family, whom I have come to rely on for support. I won't have my mom reminding me that it's time to eat dinner or my dad asking if I need help with my homework. Also, I won't have the opportunity to hang out with my friends and for us to help each other with homework. In addition, I will have to manage my academics together with my work-study job. However, with my talents and flexibility, I shouldn't have a problem getting a job. I am a very positive person who sees the good in others, so I don't think I'll have a problem making friends, and I will still have my family to give me moral support. My anxiety really borders on excitement. I can't wait to get to college and experience the change.

In this answer you show a clear understanding of the challenges of college and the value you put on friends and helping people. You also show your personality and your interest in meeting people. And most of all, you are very positive.

#4 Have you visited the colleges to which you are applying?

Bad Answer: Not yet. I don't think I need to.

Bad Answer: No. I'm waiting to see which schools accept me.

Bad Answer: I did but I found them all to be pretty much the same.

These answers do not show your interest in any college or your desire to see what the campuses look like. Remember, if you have a chance to visit the colleges to which you are applying, do so!

Bad Answer: I have visited some of the schools, including this one. I loved the campus and thought the people were friendly. That's why I want to go to this school.

Your love of the campus shouldn't be your reason to attend a school. Also, keep in mind that the people you meet during a campus visit and tour are selected for their roles because of how friendly and welcoming they are. It doesn't mean all the students are like that.

Good Answer: I haven't yet had the chance to visit any schools but I plan to do so. When I make the visits I know what I will be looking for. I want a campus that is easy to navigate and also has a variety of dorm options—singles, roommates and suites. I want to be able to enjoy the outdoors and take long runs on campus. I am hoping to be in a dormitory situation that will give me exposure to upperclassmen during my first year, if possible.

You would want to be sure that the school meets these expectations.

Great Answer: I have visited many schools but this school's campus really stood out. I felt like a visitor on the other campuses, but at this school I could picture myself as a student living in the dorms and attending classes. I just felt at home. The different options within the dorms was just what I am looking for. The layout of the campus is perfect for my morning runs. Unlike other schools with similar campuses, this school is close to a major city, which I had a chance to see during my visit. All this, together with the academic options open to me, make this school ideal.

Great Answer: I have not visited all the schools, nor do I think I'll be able to because of time and money constraints. Unfortunately, I have not had the opportunity to visit this college, much as I would have liked to. I did check out the website and talk to past and present students, so I have some idea what to expect on the campus. I like the dormitory options, the different meal plans offered and the fact that there are running trails. The schools' proximity to the city is great and would give me the opportunity to take advantage both of the city and the seclusion of the campus. I'm curious; how would you describe the campus, and what aspects of it do you think make it special?

Here you explain why you hadn't visited but give a clear understanding that you've done your research to learn about the campus. You also end the answer with a great opportunity—to ask the interviewer to tell you about the campus and what makes it unique.

#5 Why do you want to go to this school?

Bad Answer: I have friends who went there and they said it's fun.

Bad Answer: I hear it's a good school.

Bad Answer: It's a good school and it's far away from my family (or, it's close to home).

Bad Answer: My mother went there.

Bad Answer: I think I will meet some very smart people.

None of these answers is about you. The answer should reflect what is unique and special about the school, what you are looking for in a school and why this school is a good fit for you.

Good Answer: I am interested in art history, and I understand that this school has a good art history department, with a wide range of courses in the major. The school is close to the city, so I would have access to museums. There aren't many schools that can offer the great curriculum and the location. It's just what I'm looking for.

Good Answer: I want a school that has a diverse student body and isn't too far from my home in Pennsylvania. This school attracts a broad range of students; I see that there are students from twenty-five states and from twelve different countries. There aren't many schools that can say that. This school is also small enough for me to be able to interact with many of those students. I also like the classes that are offered in the psychology major, including ones in sociology and human behavior. The school's curriculum in this field is robust and will help prepare me for my future career as a child psychologist.

Great Answer: I am interested in majoring in psychology and ultimately becoming a child psychologist. It's important to me that the school I attend has a strong psychology department and an excellent track record for student admission to graduate school. This school offers a broad range of classes that will prepare me to go directly into graduate school. The psychology department's curriculum is incredible and has one of the most diverse lineups of classes that I have seen, offering everything from basic psychology to classes in sociology and human behavior. I also like the fact that the school encourages students to take classes outside their majors. This school will also help me get local internships during my junior and senior year, which I think will be critical as I proceed with my education. This school has everything I am looking for and offers opportunities that I couldn't get anywhere else.

This answer tells the interviewer that you have a clear understanding of your major and what you want to do after college. The answer points out the unique things the school offers and how those things match your interests.

Great Answer: This college has everything I'm looking for in a school: A wide range of majors and classes; an experienced and high-quality faculty; the opportunity to be in a big city; and the opportunity to engage with a diverse student body. There are few, if any, other schools that offer all those things. Having visited the school, I can definitely see myself on the campus and being a part of the student body, with all the clubs and activities. I also believe that I can bring a lot to the campus—a different perspective than others, since I come from such a small town.

This answer addresses what makes the school unique and connects those things to your interests. Don't forget—it's about you. Even talking about the school needs to be about you.

#6 I know what this school will offer you, but what will you bring to the college/campus?

Bad Answer: I can't think of anything.

Bad Answer: My sense of humor. I am really funny.

Bad Answer: I play soccer and I'm a good friend.

Bad Answer: I will start a video club if there isn't one.

These answers don't tell the interviewer what is unique and special about you and don't connect your skills, interests and background to how you'll fit in at the school.

Good Answer: I will bring my unique perspective, having read so many of the classics in high school and on my own. I love twentieth-century literature and appreciate the works of John Steinbeck, Ernest Hemingway and F. Scott Fitzgerald. My immersion in these classic works has given me a unique perspective on the transformation of literature in America, and I hope to bring that perspective to the classes in my major related to twenty-first-century theater, film and literature.

Great Answer: What I will bring to college is my appreciation for what this country has to offer and for what I have been given. I was born and raised in a small, remote town in the middle of the country, with fewer than 5,000 people. My experiences are very different than those of students who come from big cities. My entire high school has fewer students than the average grade in a city school, so how I relate to my classmates is very different than how most high school students relate to theirs. Small-town living drives a strong community but also challenges a person's ability to try new things. While I might not be viewed as worldly according to some people's definition, I think I could bring a different perspective. I look forward to trying new things with new friends and to exchanging ideas and views on politics, religion and so much more.

Great Answer: I will bring a perspective that's different from that of most other students. I believe there is something unique in every person. We come from different environments and have had different experiences, and those experiences have had a tremendous impact on who we are as people. For example, my family's history and culture are a big part of my life, having grown up in a different country. The observances and practices are beautiful and filled with tradition. I have always enjoyed sharing my background with others and learning about theirs. At this small, rural liberal arts school I believe I could be a source of education to others and a point of reference for understanding diversity. Coming from a large, closely connected family, I am fascinated by how people relate to each other and how they interact with others who are similar or very different.

This answer talks about family, tradition and experiences you've had that others have not. It points out how and why you would add to the campus life. Rather than discussing specific leadership qualities or academic accomplishments, this answer highlights your maturity and understanding of your place in the world and shows an appreciation for the opportunities you have received.

#7 What type of career or job do you want?

Bad Answer: I don't know.

Bad Answer: I want to be a lawyer, like my mom.

Bad Answer: I want to do research and find the cure for cancer.

These answers, while perhaps true, do not represent you or the thought you've given to this topic. Students have told me that they want to be a doctor and cure cancer or make prosthetics (artificial limbs) for all the children in the world who need them. While these students might have these lofty goals and the heart that goes along with them, these answers don't give a sense of who they are as people or demonstrate the confidence to make the interviewer believe that they understand the path to their objective.

Good Answer: All my life I have been exposed to lawyers, as there are many in my family. Both my mom and dad are lawyers, and so are my grandmother and my aunt. They all tell me that I think like a lawyer, but I'm not sure exactly what that means. I think it means that I get into the details and look at problems from many different perspectives. If so, that really describes me. Based on what I know about the law and the types of jobs that would be available to me, I am considering becoming a lawyer. I will likely major in history, which I think will give me perspective and help me appreciate the legal profession.

Great Answer: At this point I plan to be a doctor and would like to find a way to do both clinical work and research. I love the idea of working directly with patients. I am empathic and caring, so I think I'd be a great clinician. I also love to take on challenges and solve problems, so also being able to do research would be very rewarding. So if I can find a way to do both, I believe it would give me some great balance. I also know that there is so much about the field of medicine that I don't know and that there are so many options available to me. Attending college, particularly this one, will give me the opportunity to understand and assess my interests and abilities and will help me make clearer decisions about my future work and career opportunities.

Here you note some of your character traits and your interest in people and research. You show that you have given thought to what you want to do but are also open to learning new things and considering other options.

Great Answer: I don't know yet, but I'm hoping that the breadth of courses I plan to take my first year or two will help me narrow my focus. I do know the subjects I enjoy and am good in as well as the subjects that I find challenging. I enjoy literature and history but I struggle with math and science. I enjoy novels about young people facing life challenges, particularly those that address mental illness, as I believe we need to raise awareness in order to drive change in perception and legislation. I enjoy a good intellectual debate with my peers and with adults. This is likely because I am an only child and was included in adult activities and adult conversation my whole life. With my love of literature and social interaction, I will likely end up working in the social sciences, in the treatment of mental health or perhaps in education. This college has highly regarded sociology and psychology departments, which will enable me to explore career opportunities further. I am really looking forward to the college experience to help me make decisions about my ultimate career.

#8 Tell me about your interests and hobbies and any extracurricular activities in which you are involved.

After "Tell me about yourself," this is the most open-ended question possible. Here is your time to shine. This is your time to talk about yourself and tell the interviewer about your leadership skills, persistence, commitment, expertise, positive attitude, resilience, resourcefulness (and the list goes on) and all the unique and exceptional things about you. Don't be modest or shy, but don't exaggerate, boast or lie.

Bad Answer: I play tennis and the piano.

Bad Answer: I like to play video games.

Bad Answer: I like to watch movies and play video games.

Good Answer: I love tennis and I've been playing all through high school. I have been president of the school tennis club for the last two years. I also play the piano. I've been taking lessons since I was five years old and I play well. I like to play classical music but I'm beginning to get into jazz. I want to continue my lessons and expand the range of music I play. This is something I'm hoping to continue in college; I might even join a classical music ensemble.

Great Answer: I play many sports, but my favorite is tennis; I love the game and have been on the tennis team all through high school. I enjoy playing the game and teaching others how to play, especially beginners. Because I understand the fundamentals of the game, I can easily help someone who is learning it for the first time. I am very patient, which is another reason I believe I am a good teacher and coach. When I first started, as a freshman, I wasn't very good, but I practiced as often as I could and asked for help from the more-experienced players. I was really committed to getting better.

When I'm not playing tennis I enjoy playing the piano. I've been fortunate to have taken lessons since the age of five, and I love to play classical music. I'm hoping to join a band or start one in college. Even though I don't want to major in music, I plan to take classes in the music department—there are a lot of classes offered, and I hope to learn more about music theory.

This answer talks about your commitment, your passion, your positive attributes—such as patience, resourcefulness and focus—as well as an appreciation for what you have. It isn't so much about what you like to do, but rather, about why you like to do these things. Assuming you didn't find the information on the school website, later in the interview you can ask if there are tennis courts on campus that are available for students to use and if there are any music groups that perform.

#9 What is your favorite book?

Bad Answer: I don't like to read.

Bad Answer: Do you mean a book that I had to read for school?

Bad Answer: That's a tough question, I'll have to think about it.

These are actual responses from candidates I've interviewed. As you can see, none of these responses answers the question.

Good Answer: My favorite book is *The Color of Water*, by James McBride. It's a non-fiction book that juxtaposes the life stories of a young man and his mother.

Your objective is to give the name of a book—even one from when you were a preteen—and its author and be able to explain what the book is about and why it is important to you. But you don't want to tell the whole story, just enough so your reason for liking it makes sense. Reasons could include the connection you felt with interesting characters, the learning of a life lesson, the understanding it gave you on a particular topic, the effect it had on your perspective or even the quality of the writing.

Great Answer: My favorite book is *The Color of Water* by James McBride, which I have read many times and recommended to many people. In this memoir McBride describes, in alternating chapters, the story of his mother's life experience growing up in a Jewish home and marrying an African-American pastor, and his story of growing up in a bi-racial household. The book taught me a lot about US history and the civil rights movement. I also saw how in one family traditions kept people together while in the other family traditions broke them apart. The stories were a real inspiration to me. I connected with them as I thought about my grandparents and how they grew up, and it gave me the confidence to talk to my grandmother about her life experiences. I highly recommend the book.

Great Answer: My favorite book is a Pulitzer-prize winning book called *The Bridge of San Luis Ray* by Thornton Wilder. It takes place in the 1700s and tells the story of five people who die when a rope bridge collapses in Peru. A priest who witnesses the collapse investigates the lives of the people who were killed in order to understand what brought them to be on that bridge at that particular time. I was fascinated by the priest's desire to explore his faith and to see God's presence in everyday events. This book had a profound effect on me. It was the first time I was exposed to, and understood, the inner conflict people experience in their quest for God. It forced me to reevaluate everything I had learned about religion until that point. I also began to think about my own faith and the faith of others, within a religion and between religions. It helped me to formulate meaningful questions on the subject and to seek my own answers. May I ask, what is your favorite book?

> *This response answers the question by naming a book with a brief description of the storyline. The response explains why the book is important to you as a person and how it made you reevaluate what you had been taught, and it ends with a question that shows your intellectual curiosity.*

#10 Do you have a role model or someone you look up to?

This is one question that frustrates many interviewers no matter what school they represent. Students often say their mother or, on occasion, their father. Really? Your parents are supposed to be your role models.

Bad Answer: My sister.

> *This isn't much better than "My mother." Note: These could be good answers if your parent or sister is a truly extraordinary person and you explain why.*

Good Answer: I look up to my basketball coach. He is a great guy and spends a lot of time helping us practice and be better at the game. He pushes us hard, but it's because he wants to make us a better team. He also cares about us as students and makes sure we focus on our education as well.

Great Answer: My biology teacher is a role model to me. Even when students don't understand the subject or topic, he always stays calm and patiently tries to teach the lesson a different way. I see that other teachers, in this situation, seem to get frustrated and give up. What I realize is that he respects us, which showed me how important respect can be when interacting with other people. He also has a methodical approach to solving problems, both in biology and in general. He has taught me that if I can clearly articulate the problem I can develop a plan to solve it. He has helped me do this not only with my school work but also with my personal problems. He is a real mentor to me and has agreed to continue to be my mentor even when I go to college.

This answer identifies a specific person and explains what you admire about him and what you've learned from him. That is what a role model does; they model the behavior you'd like to exhibit. You also pointed out that you have asked him to be your mentor and secured his commitment for the coming years. You are showing that you are focused on your future and have made a commitment to this relationship. For this answer, you could just as easily talk about your guidance counselor or piano teacher or camp counselor or even a politician. What's important is that you name someone. Instead of saying the person is patient or methodical, you could just as easily say the person inspired you to try new things, or they taught you to accept failure graciously. There are so many traits and probably a lot of different people you can talk about when answering this question.

Great Answer: My physics teacher is a true role model for me. She worked as a chemist for many years and went into teaching when she retired. She inspires me with her passion for the subject and her pure love of learning. She encourages us to ask questions and to explore and learn on our own through hands-on activities. She really cares about the students and gave up her spare time to lead our school's robotics club. Through her I have seen the value of education and what real commitment looks like. She has inspired me to try my best, to value learning and teaching, and to acknowledge what I don't know and strive to learn it. In fact, her passion for teaching encouraged me to create and now run a computer workshop for students in middle school to get them excited about robotics.

Asking the Questions

Now it's your turn to ask the questions. The questions you ask the interviewer must be thoughtful ones; too often I have seen candidates struggle to think of something to ask me. It seems painful to them and it's incredibly frustrating for me. If you really don't have anything to ask in order to learn more about the college, don't ask anything. But, don't worry, I'll help you with the questions you will ask, and they will be very thoughtful.

Before we talk about what questions to ask, let's think about the person who is interviewing you. For alumni, you will focus on their experiences and perspective. Knowing some basic information about the alum will help you determine the questions to ask—and the questions not to ask. If you are asking an admissions officer, you'll need to adjust the questions a bit.

"Older" Alumni (i.e., those who graduated before or around the turn of the century)

"Technology" means something different to these alumni. They likely didn't have personal computers or mobile phones in college. Their experiences in the areas of internships, student-professor communication and even classroom teaching were very different from what you'll experience.

Don't ask these alumni to describe their internships to you, as they probably didn't have any. You, on the other hand, will likely have the opportunity to have an internship, as social media now enables companies and schools to connect. Instead, you can ask if the interviewer has any advice for a first-time intern.

Don't ask these alumni about the relationships they had with their professors. It is likely that, other than class hours or the occasional visit during office hours, they didn't see or speak to their professors. You, on the other hand, will interact with and be personally connected to your professors, virtually and in real time, via email and texts on a regular basis. Your social interaction with your fellow students will also be different than it was decades ago. You could ask if they know about how students and professors stay connected at this school, but don't be surprised if they can't shed any light on the subject.

Don't ask about the teaching styles of professors or the alum's experience with coursework. These pre-millennium alumni had to rely primarily on assigned textbooks and the professors' lectures. You now have access to large amounts, and various types, of information, so how professors teach is very different. The use of class time and the assignment of homework are different experiences now than they were in the past.

What you can ask these older alumni is to tell you about the school's history and its evolution. They can share the school's traditions and describe the ways in which the school has changed over time. This might give you an idea as to how the school adapts to change and, therefore, how it will meet your needs and expectations.

"Younger" Alumni (i.e., those who graduated in this century)

The college experience of these "millennials" will more closely resemble yours. They will be able to describe their internships, the positives and negatives associated with virtual communication with the professors, and what the classes and homework assignments were like. They can also tell you about student life on and off campus and the ways in which students meet and interact with each other. Be sure to ask them about these things.

If the interviewer didn't give you their graduation year when they contacted you, then you'll need to do some basic research. You can look them up on LinkedIn or Google them. You should be able to find out their age and their profession and calculate their year of graduation. Once you've learned something about your interviewer you can bring it up during the interview, but be appropriate and respectful. Remember that applicant who researched me online but provided little information relevant to my job or my college experience? It was odd and a bit creepy and added nothing to the interview.

Now that you know when the interviewer graduated, you can determine the appropriate questions to ask. Remember, they can only talk about themselves and their experiences, so don't ask them to answer for the entire student body, the faculty or the admissions office. And don't expect them to know the courses required for a particular major or the specifics of a class syllabus.

A Few More Tips

Whatever you do, don't ask questions just for the sake of asking or because you think it will make you seem like you are interested. Any good, experienced interviewer will see right through this. And stay away from basic, statistical, general-knowledge questions that you could have answered by looking at the college's website.

While you don't want to ask where the college is located (you should already know that), you can ask what advantages the interviewer thinks the location provides. Don't ask about the size of the student body, but you can ask what the implications are for a college that has that number of students—how the size affects the personal attention each student receives, for example. This will show that you have done your homework and will demonstrate your interest in the academic environment.

Think about the conversation you've had up until this point and the questions you've been asked and assess whether a topic that was discussed requires more explanation, information or attention. If the interviewer mentioned something that struck you as interesting or resonated with you, perhaps you can ask a follow-up question on that topic. You'll have to go with your gut and figure out the best course of action and the right follow-up questions you should ask.

People like to talk about themselves, so it's always a good idea to ask the interviewer about him/herself and his/her experiences. Don't pry into their private life, but you do want to get their perspective and thoughts around college in general and this college in particular. Don't just read from a list of questions. Think about what you are asking and whether it's appropriate for this interviewer. Think about whether you have already discussed the topic or if the interviewer couldn't possibly know the answer. And don't forget to think about when the interviewer graduated.

Note that I have included the word "generally" in some of the questions. This is to remind you that the alum cannot answer for every professor, student or graduate. What they can do is give you their perspective and describe what things were like for them when they attended college. After you've asked them about their specific experiences, you can follow up with a question about what they think your experience might be. You will need to decide about these follow-up questions based on the answer they give.

Please don't ask about things that don't interest you. Interviewers know when you are doing that, and we don't appreciate it. Ask about sports and clubs if you are interested in sports and clubs. Ask about student life if you really want to know. If there is something you have researched and learned, but want to ask their opinion, tell them you're aware and want their opinion. The asking of questions, by you of them, is a dialogue, not an interrogation.

10 Questions You Can Ask

Here are just a few basic questions you could ask the interviewer:

1. Why did you decide to go to this college?

2. Do you think that going to this college, as opposed to any other, made a difference in your career path or career opportunities? If so, how?

3. What advice would you give an incoming college freshman, specifically one attending this college?

4. How did your education and experience at this college prepare you for the job you have now?

5. This school is well-known, with a great reputation. Do you think attending this school made a difference in your ability to secure a job and subsequent promotions and career moves?

6. What is your most vivid memory of your college years? Was it a positive memory or a negative one?
   This is a great question to open the dialogue on the alum's experiences and get a sense of what stuck with them through the years.

7. The college website describes various clubs, organizations and associations on campus. What was your experience seeking out these opportunities and what advice would you give to make the process easier?

8. Which college class and professor had the greatest influence on you and why?

9. What is your favorite school tradition?
   This is a good lead-in question to learn about the alum's experience and also a way to learn about what the school stands for or is known for. Think about whether the tradition is associated with academics,

social responsibility, community involvement—or is it just something fun? If you learned about a school tradition during your research, you can ask the alum how they experienced it personally.

10. What do you think the school can do for me that no other school can?

Additional questions can be found in the Appendix.

Don't forget that communication goes two ways. The interview is not only for the school to learn more about you but for you to learn more about the school. Ask the questions that will help you decide if this is the right school for you. Find out what it's like to be a student there and figure out if you'll fit in. Is the opportunity to do research important to you? Then ask about it. If you typically need help when learning new topics, ask about what type of help is available. If you are interested in writing for the school paper, make sure there is one.

Questions You Should NOT Ask... and What to Ask Instead

All the questions listed below are ones I was asked during interviews. I have suggested alternate questions if you really need to bring up that particular topic.

Does the college have a fitness center?

You could share that you are really into body building and are impressed by what you know/saw related to the fitness center/gym. You could ask if the alum used the facility and what their experience was.

Is the school really that hard?

You could say that you know the academics at this school are challenging and ask the alum if the academics were harder than expected.

Is it easy to make friends at this school?

You could say that you are a bit of an introvert and making friends takes more time and effort for you. You could ask the alum to share his experiences or talk about the ways students interacted and ask how the administration supports freshmen through this experience.

Is there a Spanish club?

You could say that you have a love for the Spanish language and would like to participate in a Spanish club in order to keep up your knowledge of conversational Spanish. You weren't able to see clubs listed on the school website so you wondered if the alum knows about language clubs, in general, on campus.

Is there a video club?

Same as above.

Do students have to take any required courses?

You should know this from your extensive research, but you could either talk about the required classes (which you should mention by name) or ask how students manage their personal schedule if no specific classes are required.

How many students are in the freshman class?

You already looked this up. You could say you like the fact that there is a small class size, noting the number of students in the current freshman class. Or you could say you like the fact that the freshman class is large (saying the number) and so diverse. Then you can ask what the alum's experience was with such a small (or large) class size.

Can you tell me about the study-abroad program?

You already looked this up. You can ask the interviewer if she took advantage of the study abroad program and, if so, what her experience was.

Can you tell me about the school's diversity?

You already looked this up. You could mention what you learned and ask if the diversity of the student body had a large influence on the alum's experiences. You could ask an older alum if the diversity of the student body has changed over time and what he thinks the impact has been on the school.

What are the dorms like?

You looked up what you could. You can ask about what the dorm-room selection process was like or if the alum recommends a particular dorm.

Is it true that some of the introductory science classes have 300 students in one lecture hall?

While you might not be able to find this out online, perhaps you heard it from someone. You could say another alum (or a current student) told you about a very large lecture hall with seating for 300 students. You could ask the interviewer if he took classes in that room, and if so, what it was like. You could ask if the school has many lecture halls that size and if it's common for freshmen to be in such large classrooms.

Do you give money to the college?

There is no good way to ask this, nor is it any of your business.

Interviewers Who Interview Badly

Unfortunately, there is always a chance that you will get a "bad" interviewer. While it isn't very likely that you will face any of the scenarios below, if you are prepared for the worst you'll be able to handle anything.

What if the interviewer:

Doesn't ask interesting, inquisitive, open-ended questions?

Begin your questions with statements that tell about your interests and extra-curricular activities.

Doesn't follow up on your responses with more questions or doesn't engage you in two-way conversation?

Use your follow-up questions to ask them about the subject and try to encourage two-way conversation that way.

Asks mostly "yes" or "no" questions?

Answer the question with a "yes" or a "no" and immediately continue with the "why," "how" or "when" of your answer.

Tells you that your answer to a particular question is very important or, worse, critical to your possible admission?

While there is no special way to answer a question, keep in mind that no one question will be the one critical to your admittance to this college.

Shows up late, rushes you through the interview or ends abruptly?

Remain calm and don't be flustered when the interviewer shows up late. The tardiness could have been caused by something out of the interviewer's control, and you need to be understanding and respectful. If you don't have enough time to cover everything or the interview ends abruptly, use the thank-you note (see Chapter 13) to cover what you couldn't during the interview and be sure to still thank the interviewer for the time they spent with you.

Seems frustrated with your answers or impatient with the time it takes you to answer?

Try to remain calm and continue to be yourself. You are presenting the best possible you, so don't let the interviewer push you off course or disrupt your focus.

Is argumentative and challenges many of your answers?

Think of it as a way to show your open-mindedness. If the interviewer doesn't agree with something you've said, feel free to ask him to elaborate on his opinion, noting that you're interested in learning and hearing about other people's perspectives.

Asks you something "inappropriate," such as, "Are you Hispanic?" or "Are you gay?"

Although it is illegal for an interviewer to ask you about your national origin, they can legally ask you about your sexual orientation and, in fact, some colleges do so right on their application. In general, the point of asking about your sexual orientation is to let you know that they are open to accepting students of all orientations and are focused on improving their outreach to the LGBT community. It's okay to tell the interviewer that you aren't comfortable answering the question. Many seventeen-year-olds will give that same answer. As for national origin, the best advice is to answer the question. You could follow up with a question about if and how national origin plays a part in the admissions decision, if at all. You want to be respectful, so don't say, "Why does that matter?" or "Why do you care?" If you think the interviewer has been inappropriate by asking a question or in a response to your answer, you might consider contacting the school's admissions department.

In addition to all of the above, you could give a final statement that outlines your interests, experiences and character strengths and that lets the interviewer know what you can offer the school.

Throughout the difficult questions and the challenging interview, remember your relaxation exercises: take deep breaths, smile and try to stay calm. You will need to be creative and might need to find new and different ways to get your ideas and messages across.

No matter what happens or what the interviewer throws at you, remember that *it's about you.* Stay focused on what you know, what you bring to the table and what you will contribute to the school and campus life. Show your determination by making sure you get your statements made and your points across. Show the interviewer your confidence by not breaking under pressure. And don't forget to ask them about themselves and the school.

The only thing you'll be able to "control" during the interview is how you present and represent yourself. Stay focused on your message so that, no matter what, you can leave the interview knowing that you did everything you could to make it a success. That is really all you can do.

12

The Videoconference Interview

Although not many colleges offer videoconference interviews, this will change over time, and the video interview will become more prevalent. If admissions officers or alumni could interview students without leaving the comfort of their homes, this might very well catch on as a way to increase the number of interviews that can be conducted. If you are offered a videoconference interview, now or in the future, here are a few tips to be prepared and ace this interview as well.

Dress

Even though the interviewer will only see you from the waist up, dress as you would for a face-to-face interview. This will help you present the best possible you. Dressing more appropriately for the interview will make you sit up straighter, exude confidence, be more focused and show how seriously you take the interview.

In terms of what to wear, go with solid colors if possible. Try to avoid patterns or stripes, as these might be distorted in the video transmission. Similarly, avoid bright colors that might be distracting. Soft hues in button-down shirts or blouses work well.

Background

When you decide where to sit and where you will place the camera, give some thought to what will be behind you. Since you will likely be sitting at a table or desk, make sure it isn't in front of a window; the rear lighting might distort how you look or make it difficult to see you, or something might happen outside the window that is more interesting to the interviewer. A plain wall is fine, as is one with a picture or a plant, but be careful with bookshelves, as these can be distracting if the interviewer can see the names of the books.

The Camera

Position the camera so it isn't pointed up at the ceiling or cutting off the top of your head. Set the camera and your seat height so that you take up the majority of the frame and are centered. The challenge with videoconferencing is that it is difficult to make eye contact with your interviewer. Look right at the camera, not at the small image of yourself in the corner. If you are someone who tends to look away during conversations, make an extra effort to stay focused on the camera.

During one videoconference interview I conducted the candidate kept looking over to the right. I asked him what he was looking at in the front, right corner of the room. As I already knew, he wasn't looking at anything; he just tended to look away when he had a conversation. I explained that because he kept looking elsewhere, it might have led me to think that there was something or someone off-camera that was causing a distraction. With a little coaching from me he was able to continue the discussion without looking away. You certainly don't want the interviewer to think there is someone else in the room, just out of view of the camera, who is listening or helping you.

Lighting and Sound

Make sure the lighting makes you look as good as possible. Front lighting is best, rather than backlighting or indirect light. Check your sound for volume and clarity to both hear and speak. I interviewed a woman who could barely hear the questions and used that as an excuse for not answering well. You want it to sound like you are sitting next to each other.

Practice

Since videoconferencing might be new to you, you will need to practice, so ask a friend or family member to help. Set up a "real" interview with questions and answers where your friend is remote and playing the part of the interviewer. Put on your interview clothes, sit at a desk or table, in front of a wall with few distractions. Check your camera, your lighting and your sound clarity. With experience, you will master this meeting method.

Each time you have a videoconference interview, be sure to set up the technology in advance and make sure everything is in working order. Whether it's Skype, Facetime or any other web-based face-to-face program, make sure your connection is working and your camera is on. This isn't something you want to worry about at the start of the interview.

CHAPTER SUMMARY

The Videoconference Interview

Prepare ahead of time:

- Dress
- Background
- Camera
- Lighting and sound

Practice with a friend

13

Closing the Interview

B y the time the interview is over, be sure you have secured the interviewer's contact information, including email address. Send a thank-you message—either a note or an email—within twenty-four hours. In this message, you'll thank him for taking the time to meet with you and for sharing his experiences and answering your questions. Take the opportunity to remind him of something you discussed or said during the interview that differentiated you.

Reflecting back on some of my previous examples, your note might say, "I hope you had a chance to watch and enjoy my YouTube video." Or, "I am so looking forward to pursuing my love of history and joining the tennis team at this school."

CHAPTER SUMMARY

Closing the Interview

- Get their email address
- Send a thank-you note
- Re-emphasize your excitement about the school

14

Putting It All Together

You should now be ready to put all you've learned to the test. Now is the time to start practicing. Think about the school that you most want to attend and assume you are being interviewed by that school. Be sure you have done all your research and that you know all about the curriculum, the student body and the campus. Make sure you have a sense of the culture and the overall atmosphere of the college.

Next, think about *you*. What is it about you that makes you different and unique? What do you want the interviewer, and the admissions committee, to know about you? Why should the school admit you, and what will you bring that no one else can?

Think about who might be interviewing you (assume a recent graduate) and think about the questions you want to ask. Write them down on a piece of paper. Put this paper with the rest of your interview kit—pen, writing pad and anything you might want to leave behind.

Put on your best interview clothes and ask a friend or family member to interview you. Pay attention to your speed of speech and your use of slang and phrases such as "like," "um" and "yeah." Shake the person's hand, introduce yourself and maintain eye contact.

Ask the person to pick out five or six questions and be serious as they create this mock interview. For ease of practicing, the Appendix includes an extensive list of possible questions you might be asked, including the ones discussed in Chapter 10.

You Can Do It!

This is the part where you psych yourself up. You are fully prepared, you know what the school is looking for, you know who you are and what you want, and you know how to present yourself in the best way possible.

You can ace your college interview. Use the guidance and suggestions I've provided here and go out there and sell yourself. Any college would be lucky to have you; you just need to convince them of it. Remember—you can do it!

15

Final Takeaways

Some Things Are Out of Your Control

The decision as to whether or not a school accepts you is based on many factors. Aside from the usual ones (scores, grades, essays), the admissions committee focuses on maintaining a diverse student body. The number of students from your high school accepted in the last three years and the yield rate for those accepted will have a bearing on the committee's decision regarding whether or not to accept you. The number of students from your city and state already attending the college can also be a factor.

If you are not accepted to your first choice, don't take it personally. It's all about numbers, diversity, geography and so many other factors. You might have had the grades and scores to get in but didn't represent the diverse group of students they were looking for. Perhaps they already had a large number of tennis players but needed more saxophone players.

Remember, not everyone gets an interview and not everyone gets admitted. Don't take it personally—really!

Focus on Whether the School Is the Right One for You

Keep in mind that the interview goes two ways. Just as the alum is assessing if and how you might fit into the campus life and culture, you should be thinking about the same thing. It's more than, "Can I do well in college?" It's, "Can I do well at *this* college?" Understand that sometimes it's not a good fit.

Don't get carried away by the name of the school or the assumed prestige it has. Focus on what you are looking for and whether this school offers it. Be sure to ask the questions that will help you find out if this is the right fit for you. Ask the questions that will help you understand the culture and determine whether you'll fit in or if you even want to. Ask yourself, "Do I *really* want to go to *this* school?"

Not every school is right for every person. Don't choose a school simply because it has a great reputation; a school's reputation doesn't guarantee success later in life. Look at some of the companies you admire. You'll find that many of their top executives didn't go to Ivy League schools. They might even have gone to a school you never heard of.

Remember: It's About Me!

Finally, don't forget the big takeaway: IT'S ABOUT ME! It's about your qualities and your accomplishments—and also about what is best for *you* and what *you* want.

How you did on the interview is one of many factors that the college's admissions committee will consider. Acing the interview increases your chances of being accepted. And now you are ready to ace the interview.

Epilogue: After It's All Over

If you are accepted to the school, it would mean a lot to the interviewer to hear from you. Reach out via email, or even call them, and let them know how excited you are that you were accepted. Thank them again for giving you the opportunity to meet and interview, and let them know that you'd like to keep in touch.

And here's why: They might be able to help and guide you during your college years and perhaps even as you graduate from college and look for your first job. Put the interviewer down as person number one on your list of mentors and role models who could help you through college and beyond.

Even if you were denied admission to the school, it's okay to reach out and let the interviewer know. You could let them know what school you have decided to attend and thank them again for the time they took to meet with you. Even though you won't be attending their alma mater, the interviewer can still be a source of information and assistance. Stay in touch through your college years if they encourage it and use them as a resource if you can.

If any of the people who interviewed you isn't interested in keeping in touch after the process is over, they'll let you know. If they are receptive to check-ins and communication exchanges, take them up on the offer. Hopefully you will do the same one day—interview students for your alma mater and help college students by being a mentor and role model.

Appendix

For Your Parents

High school teachers and administrators have taught your child plenty of things to prepare them for college, such as how to write a college-level thesis or even how to run a science experiment with a write-up worthy of a professional scientific journal. Your child has been exposed to and extensively quizzed on vocabulary words, world history and classic literature. Guidance counselors (most of whom are terribly overworked) or college advisors (if the school is fortunate to have one) have tried to help them with the college application process. The counselor might have suggested colleges that would be a good match to your child's interests and those at which they might have a higher probability of being accepted. They might also have given advice on how to complete and answer questions on an application.

But, with all this preparation, there has been little to no emphasis on the college interview itself or on the importance of your child acing their interview to improve their chances of getting into the college of their choice.

While they might have been given some key pointers—such as arrive on time, dress well, be positive and pleasant, and get contact information so you can say thank you—these don't even begin to scratch the surface.

If you've read this book, you now understand what your child needs to do to prepare for his or her college interview. If your child asks, feel free to provide assistance and support through the process. Don't be insulted if they don't want your help; remember, your child is a teenager, and teenagers think they know everything. After reading this book they will have everything they need to ace their college interview.

Here are several things you can encourage your child to do if they ask for your help:

- Set up an appropriate email address
- Record an acceptable outgoing voicemail message

- Check their email and voicemail regularly
- Do their research and prepare their questions
- Practice answering interview questions
- Confirm the date, time and location of the interview
- Take their interview kit when they head out for the interview (pen and paper, questions and notes)
- Dress appropriately for the interview
- Do their relaxation exercises
- Arrive on time
- Send a thank-you note/email to the interviewer
- Follow up after they've been accepted

More Questions You Might Be Asked— and Answers

What are you looking forward to most in college?

Bad Answer: Playing video games with other kids.

Bad Answer: Volunteering in a local hospital.

These answers don't have anything to do with going to college, let alone this college. If you already volunteer in a hospital you can use a different question to tell the interviewer about your experiences and your desire to continue volunteering.

Bad Answer: Being able to decide for myself if I want to go to class or not. I hear that attending class is mostly optional.

Good Answer: I am looking forward to being on my own and being able to manage my schedule and my time. In addition to any required classes in my major, I am looking forward to taking classes in other subjects that interest me. I like the idea of having the flexibility to do homework late in the evening, which I can't really do in high school, and having the freedom to make my own decisions.

Great Answer: There is so much I am looking forward to in college; not only the challenging academics, but also the opportunity to be with students who love the subjects as much as I do. Being with others who share my interests will allow me to challenge myself more. I am excited about picking my electives and choosing classes in different disciplines. I want to take classes in history, psychology, astronomy and other areas outside my major so I can better understand what my alternative career options might be. Meeting students from around the country and around the world, and learning about different cultures, is going to be exciting. I know I'll have to manage my time well and that the work will be harder than it was in high school, but I'm ready for the challenge.

Are there similarities across the colleges to which you have applied, and how will you decide where you will go?

Bad Answer: They are all big (or small), all in urban (or rural) areas and they all get me away from my family. They are all pretty much the same.

Bad Answer: Whichever school gives me the most financial aid.

This might be true, but it doesn't answer the question.

Bad Answer: I don't know. I plan to decide when I find out where I've been accepted.

Good Answer: When deciding where to apply for college, I picked only schools that offer a degree in theater and that are located in a big city. I am very focused on what I want to pursue in my career and know that being in a city will provide me with the greatest opportunities. So I'll decide where to go after I know where I have been accepted.

Great Answer: My guidance counselor helped me narrow down the schools based on my interests. They are all small, rural schools offering a liberal arts degree. Coming from a large high school, I want to go to a small college and get away from the city. The curriculum is what differentiates the schools, and this one has the strongest focus on creative writing, which is the area I want to pursue. I'll have to visit the schools, but I've already decided that this school is my first choice.

Great Answer: When the process started I hadn't decided if I wanted to attend a large school or a small one, but I did know that I wanted to pursue a degree in theater. So all the schools offer an opportunity to learn and develop my acting skills. All of the schools also have diverse student bodies, as well as many clubs and activities. So I will decide based on which school can offer me the best education and the best opportunities for future employment. I also need to fit into the school culture. That's why I've decided that this school is my top choice [or in my top two choices] for college. It has everything I am looking for.

What are you looking for in a college?

This question is a gift. It's your opportunity to use all the information you gathered about the school...a chance to bring up what you like about the school and talk about some unique offerings. Then you can bring up your differentiators, how they match with the school and what you have to offer a college.

Bad Answer: A large student body.

Bad Answer: Small class sizes.

Bad Answer: A chance to be in a big city.

Good Answer: I want a school where I can be exposed to art and music and where I can learn about different forms of artistic expression. I want a school in a big city where I can visit different types of museums, attend concerts of classical and alternative music, and enjoy the expression of ideas through dance. I am looking for a school that allows and encourages me to learn and grow.

Great Answer: When I started my college search, I knew I was looking for a small liberal arts college, preferably not in a big city. I want a school that focuses on the student and does not have a required curriculum; that gives me the freedom to pick my classes and schedule my time. The strong psychology department at this school, with the award-winning professors and groundbreaking research, is exactly what I am looking for, as I ultimately want to pursue an advanced degree in social work. Student-body diversity, both geographic and cultural, is a must for me, as I will need to have a broad understanding of cultural differences to succeed in my career. This school has everything I'm looking for, and I hope that I have the chance to attend and take advantage of all that the school has to offer.

Great Answer: When applying to college I had a few things in mind. I want a school where I can learn a variety of subjects and also be exposed to non-academic opportunities. A school that will allow me to take classes in a broad range of areas, get involved with local conservation programs and meet people outside of my home state. I am not sure exactly what I want to major in, but I know it will be a social science, as I love to study human behavior and human interaction. I haven't had the opportunity to travel domestically or internationally and am looking forward to meeting a diverse group of students in college. My three older siblings lived at home and commuted to college, but I plan to live in a dorm to take advantage of the full college experience.

If you could go to any school, which would it be?

This is always a tricky question. While I have some admiration for the students who tell me their first choice is not the one I'm interviewing them for, I am always curious why they have selected the other school and, of course, why they chose to tell me. You can use this answer to show what you know about the school and show how you would fit in. It will also be a signal to the interviewer how serious you are about wanting to attend this school.

Bad Answer: If I could go to any school it would be the University of Hawaii, but my parents won't let me go there.

Bad Answer: I want to go to a different school but my parents want me to go here because they are graduates.

Good Answer: If I could go to any school it would be this one. The school offers me the opportunity to major in chemistry and also to minor in a subject outside the physical sciences. It offers a large campus and a diverse student body. This school has everything I am looking for in a college and I think I would fit in.

Great Answer: Based on my research and conversations I've had with alumni and current students, this school is my first choice. It has everything I'm looking for, including an urban setting, internship opportunities, the ability to take graduate-level courses and so much more. I think I would fit in on campus and I'm certain I'll be able to contribute to student life with my experience and passion for learning. If I'm fortunate enough to be accepted, I will definitely attend this school.

Great Answer: I have narrowed down my choices to two schools, of which this is one. This school has everything I am looking for and I believe I can quickly fit into the culture and dorm life. One factor that I will have to consider is which school is most affordable for my parents and me. In fact, this is the reason I didn't apply early decision to this school.

By giving this answer, you don't commit to attending if accepted but you do share that you are still very interested and that there is another school that has interested you. Financial concerns are a legitimate reason for saying the school isn't your first choice, but you need to be sure your response shows your continued interest.

Why are you interested in your selected field of study?

Bad Answer: I picked chemistry because I know it's a good pre-med major.

Bad Answer: It seems like it would be interesting.

Bad Answer: I'm good with people and with numbers.

Good Answer: I have been interested in this field for some time. I have done well and typically excelled in the related subjects. I know people who work in this area and I've had a chance to talk to them about it, and I believe I could do that type of job.

Good Answer: I am fascinated by human behavior and the reasons people do the things they do. I believe that majoring in marketing will allow me to learn the science and art behind how and why companies market and sell their products the way they do. Ultimately, I'd like to work in retail marketing, where I can interact with customers and with company employees.

Great Answer: I have wanted to be a chemical engineer all through high school. A close friend of the family is a chemical engineer, and I've enjoyed talking to her about her work. We've talked about the courses offered at this college and how well they'd prepare me for different types of jobs. Classes like process engineering and material design sound incredibly challenging and would prepare me to pursue various paths in the engineering field. The friend has given me her perspective on the difference between majoring in chemistry and majoring in chemical engineering and the choices I'd have after graduation. I know this is only one person's perspective, but I feel like I'm going in with my eyes wide open to the challenges as well as the opportunities. Ultimately, I'll be able to combine my love of math and science with my interest in business and management. This seems to be the perfect area of study for my academic interests.

If you could work for any company right now, which company would you choose and why?

Bad Answer: Google, because it's cool and the food is free.

Bad Answer: Amazon, because they are huge and I want to be in sales.

Bad Answer: Apple, because I love their products.

Good Answer: I would choose a large company that offers career growth potential so I can move up the corporate ladder. But it also has to be small enough so I can make a difference and stand out. And I have to like their products or services.

Although this answer doesn't actually name a company, it does show ambition and interest.

Great Answer: I'd work for the consulting firm Ernst & Young. They offer consulting services in diverse areas, and by supporting their clients I would have the opportunity to work with different types of companies in different industries. I'd be able to apply what I have learned while also learning from their experienced consultants. I would like to travel, and working for a global consulting firm might give me that opportunity.

Great Answer: I would work for the Walt Disney Company. With a degree in computer engineering, I would be able to apply my skills to the media and entertainment industry while working for a global leader in this space. Also, Disney is strongly committed to philanthropy and the environment, both of which are important to me.

How do your friends describe you?

The interviewer can learn more about how you might mesh with your peers on campus by the answer you give. Be sure to mention all of your positive attributes.

Bad Answer: They think I'm funny and silly.

Bad Answer: I'm the clown of the group.

Bad Answer: I'm a bit weird and a nerd but they like hanging out with me.

Good Answer: My friends would say that I am really smart and that I am always helpful. When they call for help with their homework I always take the time to help them.

Great Answer: My friends would say that I take my studies seriously and that I am always available to help them if they need it. With all the activities we do together, they would say I am a leader and a good teammate. They'd say I am decisive when decisions have to be made; good at bringing everyone together; that I get along with everyone; and that while I can be intense about my studies, I don't take myself too seriously.

How would your teachers describe you?

Bad Answer: I'm hysterical; I'm the class clown.

Bad Answer: I'm smart and I participate in class.

Bad Answer: My teachers don't really know me.

Good Answer: I'm a very good student, I work hard and I get good grades.

Great Answer: My teachers would say that not only am I a good student and someone who works hard to succeed, but that I am also a leader and a teacher in that I encourage and help others to succeed as well. I ask inquisitive questions and love to engage in dialog with my classmates, particularly when there are diverse opinions. My teachers would say they can rely on me and that when I'm asked to do something, I do it.

If you could change one thing about your high school, what would it be and why?

Bad Answer: The teachers.

This is a silly answer and not realistic.

Bad Answer: The diversity. Too many students from one geographic and socioeconomic area.

This doesn't answer the question about a change you would make, nor is it realistic.

Good Answer: I would change the hours that the school is open and when classes are offered. The students need more flexibility so they can have time available to get a job.

Great Answer: Currently the students are not able to take all the courses they want to take, especially the honors and AP classes, because of the times they are offered. Many of these classes overlap so you can't take both AP History and AP Biology. I would redesign the schedule for juniors and seniors to offer more sections of these advanced classes so the students could take all the AP classes they want.

What is your greatest accomplishment?

Bad Answer: I haven't really accomplished anything yet in my life.

Bad Answer: Well, I passed all of my mid-year exams.

Good Answer: I'm a good student and committed to the school and its students. As senior class president, I was able to make some changes in my high school; one such change was getting the school to expand the cafeteria menu to include healthier options.

Great Answer: I believe that my greatest accomplishment so far has been my role as senior class president, in which I represent the class to the school administration and the PTA. I not only get to share our grievances and concerns, but also get to be part of creating the solutions. Under my leadership, changes were made to the management of student activities, and the seniors are now given more responsibility to design and implement specific programs like the senior prom. In the past the senior class had to follow the administration's guidance and had no input in major decisions. Now, for the first time, we do.

Great Answer: My greatest accomplishment is that I got my grandparents to talk about their life and experiences before they moved to the United States. I'm not very into sports and don't have the typical accomplishments that many teenagers have. What I do have is a sense of pride in my family and my culture. While I hadn't heard many stories from my grandparents, I have a strong connection to my heritage. My grandparents on my father's side emigrated from Ecuador when they were newly married. Life was hard for them back home and they wanted a better life for their children. They worked hard and were able to support their four children through college. My father and his siblings could never get my grandparents to talk about their time in Ecuador; the children thought it was too painful for their parents to discuss. I spent a lot of time with my grandparents, just the three of us, talking about my interest in history and my desire to understand where I come from. It took months of conversation but I was finally able to get my grandparents to talk about their past. It wasn't that their memories were painful to them, it's that they were so sweet it was hard for them to think about their home country and not be able to travel there. My cousins and I now have a written and recorded history of the lives of our grandparents, something my father and his brothers thought would never happen.

If you mentioned an interest in study abroad and/or checked it off as an interest on your application (of course you made sure this school offers study abroad), you might be asked:

In what country do you want to study abroad and why?

Bad Answer: Syria, because that's where my family is from.

This is a bad answer because, I'm just guessing here, Syria is not one of the countries on the list of options for this school's study-abroad program.

Bad Answer: Any country in Africa because I want to help the poor.

Good Answer: France, because I want to learn French, and I believe that the best way to learn a foreign language is to live in the country. I would love the opportunity to be immersed in the culture, learn about the history and take advantage of other travel opportunities from there.

Great Answer: If I have the opportunity to study abroad, I would like to visit a country where I can learn the language, where there is a different culture than what we have in the United States, and where I might have an opportunity to also visit other countries. Much of Asia would be a consideration, although my first choice is Japan. It is rich in culture, ancient art and history, and while there I would be able to learn so much, particularly outside of the classroom. With my love of cooking I would try to take classes in Japanese cuisine and add it to my repertoire.

See how you've added another dimension of yourself in this answer? This might lead to follow-up questions if the interviewer is a foodie.

Practice Questions

- Tell me about yourself.

- What is your favorite book?

- What will you miss most when you go off to college?

- Do you have a role model or someone you look up to?

- Why are you interested in your selected field of study?

- What are the similarities across and differences between all the schools to which you have applied?

- What factors will you consider when making the decision on where you will go to college?

- What makes you anxious about going to college?

- What type of job or career do you want?

- Why do you want to go to this school?

- If I asked your friends to describe you, what would they say?

- Of all the schools to which you have applied, which is the one you really want to attend?

- What are you looking forward to most in college?

- Have you visited the colleges to which you are applying?

- I know what this school will offer you, but what will you bring to the college/campus?

- What are you looking for in a college?

- If you could change one thing about your high school, what would it be and why?

- If you could work for any company right now, which company would you choose and why?

- What do you enjoy most about your high school?

- How would your teachers describe you?

- Tell me about your extracurricular activities, your interests and your hobbies.

- What country are you interested in visiting for a study-abroad program and why?

- What is your greatest accomplishment?

- Tell me about a person or activity that has challenged you.

- Would you describe yourself as a leader, one of the pack or a follower? Why?

- What are your three greatest strengths?

- Tell me about someone in your life who has had a major impact on you.

- What three words best describe you? Why did you choose those words?

For those attending a private, parochial or charter high school:

- Who made the decision for you to attend your high school? If it was your parents, do you think they made the right decision? If it was your decision, what was your motivation?

Questions You Can Ask the Interviewer

- Why did you decide to go to this college?

- Did the college meet your expectations? Did it miss the mark on anything or exceed your expectations in any area?

- Do you think that going to this college, as opposed to any other, made a difference in your career path or career opportunities? If so, how?

- What advice would you give an incoming college freshman and, specifically, one attending this college?

- Do you have any regrets about your years at this college? If so, do you have advice for me as a result of those regrets?

- How did your education and experience at this college prepare you for the job you have now?

- What was your experience with internships while you were in school? Did you receive assistance in finding the opportunities, and did you get support from the faculty during the internships? *Remember, this only applies to the more-recent graduates.*

- Do you have any suggestions on internships, such as how best to secure an internship and how to decide which opportunity to take?

- I can see that you stay involved with the school through your volunteering to interview. Do you stay connected in any other way, and how does the school stay connected to you?

- This school is well-known, with a great reputation. Do you believe that attending this school made a difference in your ability to secure a job and subsequent promotions and career moves?

- It seems to me that this school is not very well known and, in fact, I've met people who've never heard of it. Do you find this too? Did the fact that it's not very well-known make it more difficult when you were looking for internships or jobs?

- What do you think is the biggest challenge faced by a college freshman today? Can you offer me advice in this area?

- What would you say are the benefits of attending a school in an urban (or suburban or rural) setting?

- Does the school have a strong alumni network, and are graduates offered a way to stay connected? Do you stay connected with your fellow alumni?

- What gives you the most pride about this college? Would you say other alumni take pride in this as well?

- What is your most vivid memory of your college years? Was it a positive memory or a negative one?

- How would you describe the general relationships between the professors and the students? What were your relationships with your professors like?

- In general, are professors available for in-person meetings and conversations, or are students encouraged to communicate with them via email or social media?

- What are the classes like? Are students allowed to use laptops in the lectures? Does the instructor use technology during the lecture? To what extent are students expected to be "connected"?

- Did you ever feel unsafe on campus?
  This question is particularly appropriate for schools in large cities where the general public might be on or near campus. This can also be used as a lead-in for a woman to ask an alumna about her experience with sexual harassment and/or the school's approach to, and tolerance of, sexual harassment.

- Did the college offer guidance related to which courses you should take?

- How would you rate the academic counseling that was offered?

- The college website describes various clubs, organizations and associations on campus. What was your experience seeking out these opportunities, and what advice would you give to make the process easier?

- Do you recommend that a student live on or off campus, and how would you answer for each of the four years of my college experience?

- Which college class and professor had the greatest influence on you?

- Which college activity had the greatest influence on you?

- Does this college offer career-planning guidance and access to internships and future jobs?

- Can you tell me about student life on and off campus and what is available to students when they are not in class or working?

- This is a college, not a university. Do most graduates typically head right into the job market, or do they go on to graduate school? If they go to graduate school, to what extent does the college help them pursue those opportunities?

- This college is part of a university. Do graduates typically head right into the job market, or do they go on to graduate school? If they go to graduate school, are they encouraged to stay within the university, and do they have a better chance of being admitted if they received their undergraduate degree from the college?

  A college offers only an undergraduate degree. A university offers undergraduate degrees through their colleges and also offers graduate degrees through their other schools. If you are interested in going to graduate school, this is a way to understand if attending this college will help your chances of getting in to one of the school's graduate programs. Note that the alum might not know unless they themselves went to graduate school.

- What would you say is the most unique attribute of this school? Did this attribute influence your decision to apply and attend?

- Were you involved in a fraternity/sorority—and if so, what was your experience? What is the general opinion of the fraternities and sororities on campus? Is joining a fraternity/sorority something you would recommend?

  A fraternity is a social group for men and a sorority is a social group for women. Men, ask about fraternities; women, ask about sororities. Some fraternities accept women, but this is rare.

- Are you still in touch with your classmates?

If the interview is with a professor or department chair, you might ask them the following:

- If you could change one thing about your department, what would it be and why?

Additional questions for admissions representatives, or professors, if appropriate:

- If you could change one thing about this school or this department, what would it be?
- What are the top three attributes the college is looking for in an applicant?
- What does this school offer that no other school does?
- What is the one thing this college wants students to take away with them after graduation?
- What does the school do in support of the alumni and to keep them connected?
- How do you know if you've been successful at your job?

Cram Guide

- Dress: neat, clean and appropriate
- Take your interview kit—paper, pen, list of questions you will ask, anything you want to share or leave behind
- Relax
- Shake hands
- Make eye-contact
- Speak slowly and clearly
- IT'S ABOUT ME!!!! Tell the interviewer about yourself
- Be positive
- Answer the question
- Ask follow-up questions and questions from your prepared list
- Show interest in the school
- Remember, the interviewer is looking for:
    - Intellectual curiosity
    - Personality
    - Interests
    - Passion
    - Values
    - Community involvement
    - Maturity
- Get contact information
- Send a thank-you note/email

Acknowledgments

My endless gratitude to Ann DeMarais, Stephanie Bash-Soudry, Lynn Kestin Sessler, Lili Brillstein, Paul O., Rona & Scott Black, Jeff & Anna Fineberg, and Deborah C—without whom this book would not have been possible.

My thanks to Hannah Sessler, Michelle Tillis Lederman, Beryl Sue Katz, Adam & Diana Hird—whose guidance, feedback and support were invaluable.

My thanks also to Janica Smith, Cathy Davis and Jack Davis for their guidance, patience and creativity in making this book a reality.

A final thanks to my husband, Ben, the best editor any writer could have, for supporting me throughout this process.

About the Author

Ethelyn Geschwind earned a B.S. in chemical engineering from Columbia University's School of Engineering and Applied Science and an MBA in Marketing from NYU's Leonard N. Stern School of Business. Ethelyn has been interviewing students applying to her undergraduate alma mater for more than twenty-five years. She also coaches high school and college students, mentors newly employed college graduates, and runs workshops to help high school seniors prepare for their college interviews and college students prepare for their job interviews.

Ethelyn lives with her husband and son in Maplewood, New Jersey. She can be reached at Ethelyn@PerfectPrep.net

Made in the USA
Charleston, SC
15 October 2016